I0128914

MARKETING MANAGEMENT ESSENTIALS

YOU ALWAYS WANTED TO KNOW

Second Edition

CALLIE DAUM

VIBRANT
PUBLISHERS

Marketing Management Essentials

You Always Wanted To Know

Paperback ISBN-10: 1-949395-79-0

Paperback ISBN-13: 978-1-949395-79-2

Ebook ISBN-10: 1-949395-80-4

Ebook ISBN-13: 978-1-949395-80-8

Hardback ISBN-10: 1-949395-73-1

Hardback ISBN-13: 978-1-949395-73-0

Library of Congress Control Number: 2018907781

This publication is designed to provide accurate and authoritative information in regard to the subject matter covered. The Author has made every effort in the preparation of this book to ensure the accuracy of the information. However, information in this book is sold without warranty either expressed or implied. The Author or the Publisher will not be liable for any damages caused or alleged to be caused either directly or indirectly by this book.

Vibrant Publishers books are available at special quantity discount for sales promotions, or for use in corporate training programs. For more information please write to bulkorders@vibrantpublishers.com

Please email feedback / corrections (technical, grammatical or spelling) to spellerrors@vibrantpublishers.com

To access the complete catalogue of Vibrant Publishers, visit www.vibrantpublishers.com

What experts say about this book!

"Marketing Management Essentials You Always Wanted to Know" is a brilliant book. My students loved the ease of reading and the relatability of the text.

> – Kristopher J. Patterson
> **Adjunct Marketing Professor, Rutgers Business School**
> **Digital Marketing Head Tutor, Yale University**
> **Senior Integrated Marketer, Wolters Kluwer Legal &**
> **Regulatory US**

Marketing Management Essentials You Always Wanted to Know is a great book and covers many of the important foundational concepts for an introductory course in marketing management. It provides a good overview of the topic.

> – Jim Lecinski
> **Associate Professor of Marketing at Northwestern**
> **University**

This page is intentionally left blank

Exciting new resources for readers:

Thank you for an overwhelming response to *Marketing Management Essentials You Always Wanted To Know*. We are committed to publishing books that are content-rich, concise and approachable enabling more readers to read and make the fullest use of them.

We are excited to announce two add-ons in this new edition of the book.

- A Chapter Summary is added at the end of every chapter. This will help to get a quick access point of what was covered in the chapter. It also assists in identifying the important information after reading through the entire chapter.

- This updated edition includes a chapter on Digital Marketing which covers search engine optimization, pay per click, email marketing, social media marketing and much more.

Should you have any questions or suggestions, feel free to email us at reachus@vibrantpublishers.com

We hope this book provides you the most enriching learning experience.

THIS BOOK IS AVAILABLE IN E-BOOK, PAPERBACK(B/W), PAPERBACK (COLOR) AND HARDBACK (COLOR) FORMAT.

BUY 3 FOR THE PRICE OF 2

USE DISCOUNT CODE 3FOR2

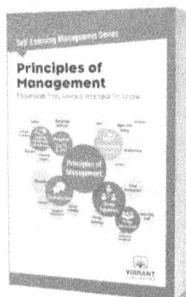

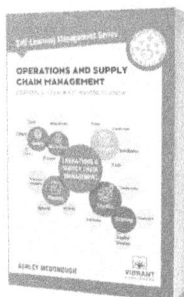

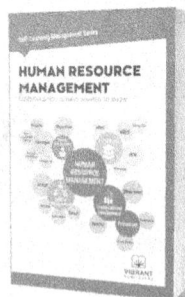

Table of Contents

About the Author

Callie Daum has worked in the healthcare industry for over 20 years gaining experience in managing teams, project management, strategic development and implementation, business marketing to increase revenues, and many more lessons learned on how to thrive in a business industry. As a seasoned Senior Project Manager and Leader, her goals include adding value, working efficiently and effectively, and sharing best practices to achieve overall success. Callie started her career as an Application Analyst at Computer Sciences Corporation, before moving on to project management and leadership at Cerner Corporation, Atrium Health, and Novant Health. Callie is a certified Project Management Professional, Professional Scrum Master, Certified Health Coach, and received a certificate in Master Level Six Sigma at Villanova University.

This page is intentionally left blank

Preface

Marketing management is a role of its own. The marketing manager is one whose skillset expands across different areas of the organization. Most people outside of the marketing realm do not have a deep understanding of what marketing managers do and what the required skillset is. Some may say they have acquired the skillset because they studied marketing in school but, again, studying and experiencing are two totally different things. So, how do you succeed in a new role of marketing manager?

Marketing Management Essentials You Always Wanted To Know seeks to guide you in answering this question. This reading consists of core elements of marketing management that will support day to day activities. New marketing managers may be faced with challenges such as conducting an external audit, forecasting demand, developing a plan to gain new customers, and ensuring other departments are playing their part in providing customer value. These items are included in this reading along with several other elements to help anyone understand and function in their role of marketing manager. Using real life experiences and detailed study, this handbook will give you the tools to get started in your marketing management role.

This page is intentionally left blank

Chapter **1**

Introduction to Marketing Management

Marketing affects everyone, every day. We all engage in marketing on a daily basis, so it is important that we understanding what marketing is. A **market** can be defined by Philip Kotler as, "…all the potential customers sharing a particular need or want who might be willing and able to engage in exchange to satisfy that need or want. "**Marketing** is a function of an organization. It is a group of processes or procedures for developing, connecting, and providing value to consumers. It is also for dealing with customer relations in ways that profit the organization and its stakeholders. Marketing is achieved by social and managerial processes. These processes consist of consumers and groups of consumers acquiring their needs and wants by developing and swapping products and value with one another. With the cut throat competitive conditions and the advancement of production, distribution, stocking and pricing as well as digitalization, marketing has become Managing Relationships with Customers, Distributors, facilitators (Banks, advertising and PR people,) partners and public at large. Marketing seeks to fulfill those wants, needs, and desires from the consumer both present and anticipated in future.

Marketing is important because in the 21st century, with the struggling economy, organizations used marketing to help keep their companies afloat. Marketing helps to tackle the challenges faced in a failing environment. In a broader sense, marketing has brought awareness of products and services to the public that have made their lives better. When marketing is successful, demand increases for an organization's products and services. It also helps to establish a brand in the public eye and build brand loyalty. Indirectly, successful marketing creates jobs for individuals because demand is increased and more assistance to produce and distribute the products and services is needed. In its simplest form, marketing puts products and services in the hands of its targeted consumers.

Marketing is an organizational function covering almost all areas of business. The following list shows the many functions in an organization that can be categorized as a marketing function.

- Customer Relationship Management (CRM)

- Display

- Stockholding

- Servicing

- Risk Taking

- Transporting

- Market Research

- Merchandising

- Publicity

- Pricing

- Forecasting

- Buying

- Financing

- Selling

- Public Relations

- Advertising

- Sales Promotion

Marketing is a management function. Management must ensure that the operations of the organization are running smoothly to ensure the customer's needs are met effectively and efficiently. Manager conduct analysis, plan, allocate resources, control current processes, and work to anticipate customer needs in an effort to ensure customers are satisfied. Additionally it tries to anticipate needs and wants of customers/ consumers in the future by evaluating the social, economic, cultural, political and technological developments.

Marketing is a business concept. Here is where the exchange process comes into play that are associated with obtaining goods and services. This is where supply and demand come in. If I have the supply and you have a demand of the product, we can negotiate a deal.

It is considered an exchange when:

- Two groups or more are involved

- Both groups have something of value that the other group desires

- Both groups effectively communicate and deliver

- Both groups have the option to turn down each other's offers

- Both groups want to negotiate with the other party

Figure 1.1

Marketing is a business philosophy. It sees the importance of the customer and that all business exists to serve customers rather than manufacturing products. Marketing takes the customer as the core of its activities. Marketing takes the customer as the core of its activities.

In the remainder of this reading we will explore these concepts and dive deeper into marketing and marketing management, so we can better understand its inner works.

Stages of Marketing

Not all marketing is greatly expensive, involving extensive research from a reputable firm and spend inordinate amounts of money on advertising and keeping up large marketing departments. Some organizations work with what they have. They stretch their current resources, maintain close relationships with customers and use information gathered to meet the customer's needs. These organizations focus on building their brand and customer loyalty and less on advertising and PR.

Not all marketing is the same. There are three phases of marketing that can occur.

Examine the illustration below that describes the phases and their definitions.

Figure 1.2

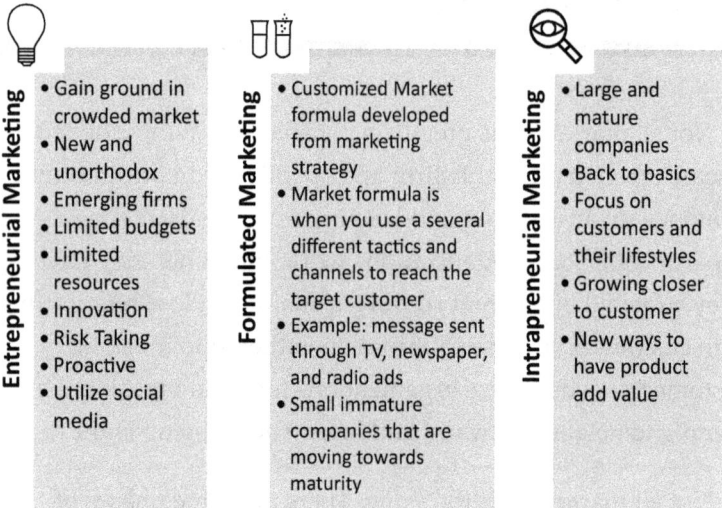

Entrepreneurial Marketing
- Gain ground in crowded market
- New and unorthodox
- Emerging firms
- Limited budgets
- Limited resources
- Innovation
- Risk Taking
- Proactive
- Utilize social media

Formulated Marketing
- Customized Market formula developed from marketing strategy
- Market formula is when you use a several different tactics and channels to reach the target customer
- Example: message sent through TV, newspaper, and radio ads
- Small immature companies that are moving towards maturity

Intrapreneurial Marketing
- Large and mature companies
- Back to basics
- Focus on customers and their lifestyles
- Growing closer to customer
- New ways to have product add value

Marketing Capacity

In the following section, let's answer the questions of who what when where and why in relation to marketing. First, what is marketed?

Figure 1.3

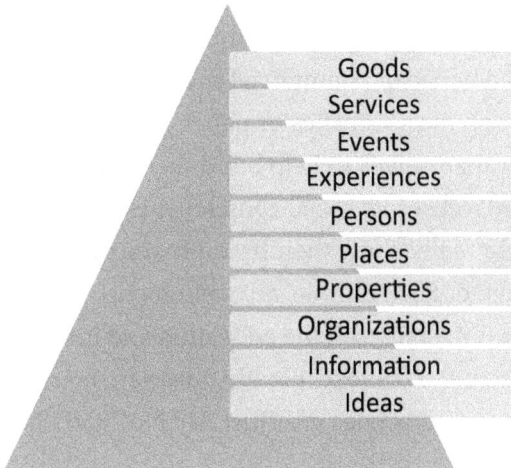

Goods are the most commonly marketed item in the list above, they are physical in nature. Examples of goods would be cars, food, clothing, and furniture. Next are services which carry a 70-30 service to goods ratio. Examples of services would be airlines, banking, and doctors. Sometimes you see a mix of goods and services such as in construction. Events can also be marketed or promoted. Examples of events would be concerts, sports events, and performances. Experiences are another item that is commonly marketed. Experiences include a coordination of several activities to provide a specific type of experience. A great example of this is Disneyworld. They orchestrate a lot of elements to provide a magical experience. It is strange to say that marketing helps to sell people. It is, however, true if you think about it in the context of an image of a person or a brand. For example, high profile plastic surgeons sell themselves through marketing to lure in new clients. A more recent marketing effort has gone into marketing places. Doing this is promoting tourism in a specific city or state. For example, there are several commercials on TV advertising California and all it has to offer. Property marketing really falls within the realm of real estate. In order to sell a house or commercial property, an agent advertises the property on local websites or papers. Organizations often advertise for themselves to help build their brand. For example, Patagonia, advertises its social consciousness and volunteer efforts to help really show their brand to the public. Information is also marketed. For example, advertisements you see for colleges and university sell the education and information you would get from that college. Finally, ideas are marketed. For example, two famous ones are "Just Say No" and "No means No".

Marketing Management

Marketing management is the discipline of selecting goal markets and attaining, possessing, and increasing customers through generating, distributing, and communicating higher customer value.

The above list is extensive and requires resources in order to properly market each of them. A marketer is responsible for developing this marketing. They are essentially looking for some sort of response from the consumer, also referred to as a prospect. If both the marketer and the prospect are wanting to sell one another something, they can both be termed marketers.

Demand Management

A marketer's largest responsibility is to create demand for the item they are marketing. Essentially, marketers are demand orchestrators or demand managers. They control how much demand, timing, and logistics. Demand managers can create demand, diminish demand, and increase or decrease demand. When they are managing this demand, they must be cognizant of the different states of demand. See the list below to explain the different states.

Demands management includes customer management. Organizations need to determine if they want to create new customers or maintain repeat customers, or both. Creating a group of new customers is a costly endeavor and hard to come by due to the ever-changing environment, economy, and competition. Due to these challenges, you will find more organizations shifting their focus to retaining their loyal customers.

Figure 1.4

Negative demand

- The product is avoided and not liked and consumers could go as far as paying to avoid it.

Nonexistent demand

- There is a general unawareness of the product by consumers are they are just not interested.

Latent demand

- There is a strong desire for the item but none of the products in the market are satisfying.

Declining demand

- Purchase of the item is less and less and eventually not at all.

Irregular demand

- Purchase of this item happens in intervals such as seasonal, monthly, weekly, etc.

Full demand

- Products in the marketplace are being purchased by consumers.

Overfull demand

- Demand for the item is greater than what is available.

Unwholesome demand

- Product possesses adverse social consequences but consumers are still attracted to purchasing the item.

If we are looking at marketing from a high level, and the industries that make up the economy as a whole, there are five different markets where demand occurs. These markets can really be thought of as different groupings of consumers. Exchange of goods, services, and information occurs between all of these markets.

Look at the diagram below to see the relationships that occur during this exchange process.

Figure 1.5

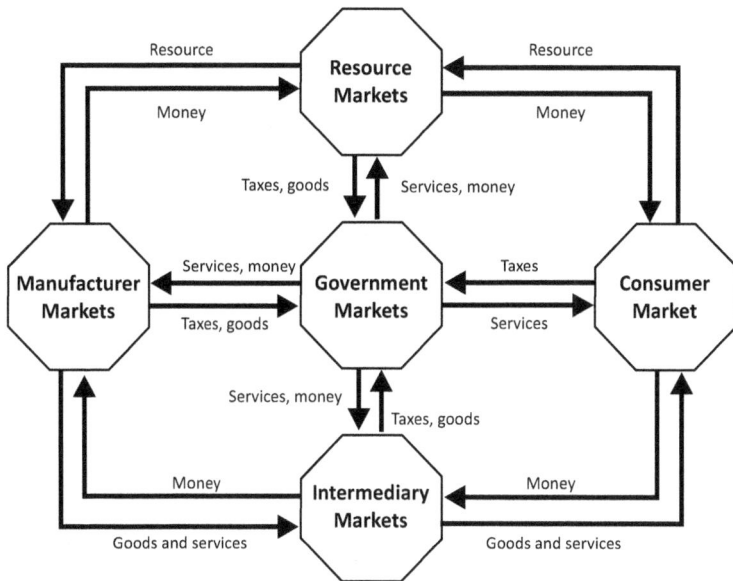

This picture demonstrates how goods and services flow through the different markets and how government is at the center of it all. Money flows through all markets while taxes come into the government from all the markets. The government provides services to the consumer with the taxes that the consumers pay. The government gives services and money to all of the markets in exchange for their taxes and goods. Goods and services flow between manufacturer, intermediary, and consumer markets. Resources come from the consumer market into the resource market and put back into the manufacturer market. This is a rather complicated big picture.

Let's take a look at how a simple exchange process works.

Figure 1.6

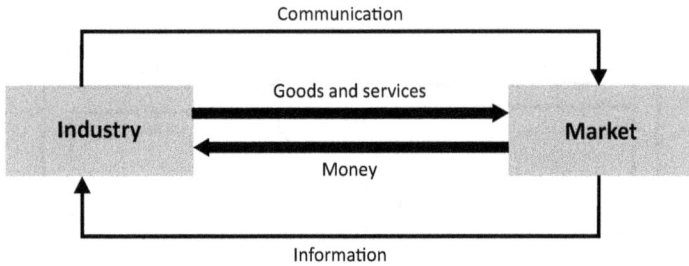

There are different types of markets these exchanges can happen in. First, the consumer market is what everyone participates in to meet their daily needs. This market consists of organizations who create and distribute consumer goods and services such as groceries and clothing. Next, there is a business market where organizations employ skilled negotiators purchase goods and services for their organizations. They also determine their competitive advantage and find different ways to demonstrate their product's value. In the global marketplace, organizations who participate have to make a lot of decisions to ensure that they are entering the right market at the right time. They must ensure they understand the culture and the needs of each of the different countries to determine which is right to enter. Organizations participating in the nonprofit and governmental markets are selling to customers who have limited resources for purchases such as churches, public schools, and charities. In the government market, sellers typically place bids to become the exclusive provider.

Figure 1.7

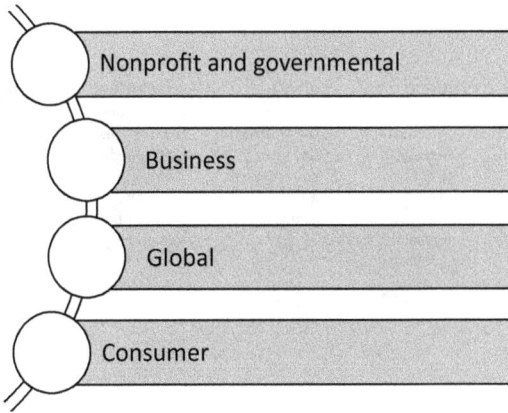

As we continue on in the reading, it is important to understand the meaning of a few terms. Marketplaces are physical places or brick and mortar locations. Marketspaces are a digital foot print. Metamarkets are products that are complementary to each other, but they are spread across markets. Metamediaries are vehicles of navigation for consumers through the metamarkets.

Philosophies

When we are in the middle of marketing management, we are completing specific activities with the goal of driving desired effects and exchanges with our target customer. The driving factor behind those marketing activities is called a philosophy. In the following section we will look at several of these philosophies including production, product, selling, marketing and societal marketing.

Figure 1.8

Production	Product	Selling	Marketing	Societal marketing
• Available products that are very affordable • Improve production • Increase distribution efficiency • One of the oldest	• Most quality, performance and features • Use energy and resources to make improvements to goods and services	• Increased selling efforts • Use energy and resources for sales campaign	• Understand the desires and needs of the target market • Deliver better than competitors in both efficiency and effectiveness	• Understand the desires and needs of the target market • Deliver better than competitors in both efficiency and effectiveness • Maintain or improve consumer and society well being

In the production concept, companies try to satisfy the demand in the market with new products. Because, there is a big demand in the market which is not satisfied with products. Early years of industrialization all efforts were directed for production. Customers were not demanding high quality stuff but basic goods to satisfy the basic needs. The founder of the US company Ford, Henry Ford introduced a car into the US market called T-Model. He said "you can choose any color you want as long as it is black". On the other side the General Motors produced colorful cars thus giving the customers a choice. Since then Ford was not able to close the gap in sales with GM cars.

In the product concept, the idea is that consumers look for products that offer high quality, performance and features. Therefore, continually improving upon the current version of the product is critical to success. This concept is based on the idea that if I build a bigger better bug swatter, consumers will come running to buy it. This is not necessarily always true, the consumer may be looking for better and more innovative way to get rid of bugs such as sprays, candles, etc. Don't fall into the trap that bigger and better equals success. Also, this concept is related to marketing myopia. Marketing myopia is where a company focuses on their needs rather than the needs and desires of the customer.

In the selling concept, the philosophy is that you will never sell enough of a product unless you undergo a big selling effort. Consumers may not be willing voluntarily to buy product perhaps they were not in need of that product. So they need to be encouraged and convinced to buy the products. Companies need to hire salesmen who can explain the special attributes of the products to the buyers. Typically, this philosophy is associate with goods that consumers don't necessarily think of buying. This is also associated with non-for-profit organizations. You don't typically think of "buying" a mayor so lots of marketing happens to keep specific candidates at the forefront of your mind. Another reason this may be used is because an organization has produced too much of a specific good, so they are looking to sell their inventory versus what the market is asking for. There is high risk involved with this marketing because it assumes that all you have to do is tell the consumer how much they need the product and they'll buy it. They may buy the product and not like it, but the assumption is they will forget they didn't like it and buy it again later. These assumptions are not necessarily grounded in factual data. In fact, research suggests that if a consumer does not like a product, they will not buy it again and they will tell their friends not to buy it either.

However after a certain period of the sales era companies faced a dilemma because the customers do not want to buy products that are produced without consultation with them. They wanted to be consulted about their needs and wants. This is called the Marketing concept. With the marketing concept, the organization needs to determine the needs, wants and desires of the target market and they must deliver effectively and efficiently. They must deliver better than their competitors. In order for this to work, everyone in the organization must be on board – from top down to bottom up. Everyone must be vested in retaining customers. For this reason, organizations spend a lot of time investing their time on how to motivate and inspire all of their team members to provide excellent customer service. Organizations must hone-in on the customers' needs and competitors' strategies. To be successful, organizations must go so far as to break down their customer population and determine each individual groups' desires, so they can meet their satisfaction requirements. In some cases, customers themselves do not even know what they want so customer driving marketing comes into play. This is where the organization learns so much about the customer that they know more about what the customer wants than the customer does. With this concept, it is important for organizations not to get so caught up into meeting customer satisfaction that they forget that it should not be met at the expense of profitability. All these philosophies reflect the historical developments in any economy. As the economic progress competition becomes more and more stiff. Because new companies enter to the market with similar or new products thus forcing the old ones change the way they compete. The only solution is to go to the customer to understand what type of needs and wants and desires they have before they start to produce.

Figure 1.9

Selling	Marketing
Start - Factory	Start - Market
Emphasis - Existing products	Emphasis - Customer needs
How - Sell and promotion	How - Integrated marketing
End - Profits through increased sales	End - Profit through increased customer satisfaction

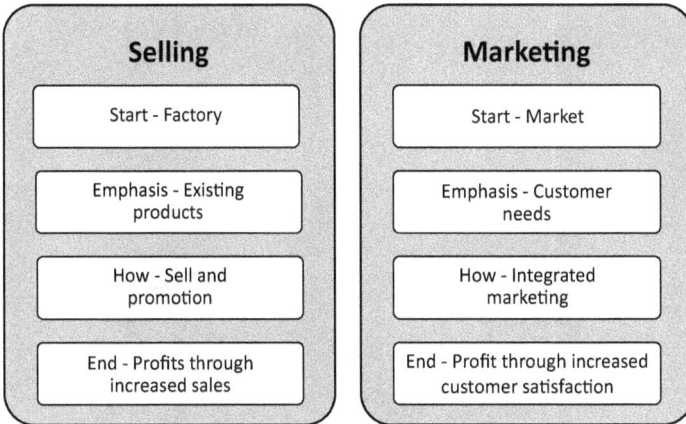

As time goes by, companies will feel the pinch of social reactions in terms of their contribution to the air and sea river, lake pollution. People start accusing the companies about their negative effects to the nature. This brings marketing new dimension: social responsibility. We call this philosophy Societal Marketing. Societal marketing is similar to the marketing concept in that they both believe that the organization should have a clear understanding of the customers' wants, needs, desires, and interests. Societal is different in that it adds an extra layer where we not only want to do it better than competitors, but we want to make sure that we are doing it in a way that sustains or improves both the consumer's and society's welfare. This philosophy is the newest emerging philosophy today. It really looks at the question, does the strictly marketing concept take into account the environment of today? For example, is using coal as an energy source socially responsible and healthy for the consumer? Or, are genetically modified products socially responsible and healthy for the consumer? Societal marketing suggests that pure marketing does not address these questions adequately. Using this concept forces organizations to really look at meeting all of societies' expectations.

Figure 1.10

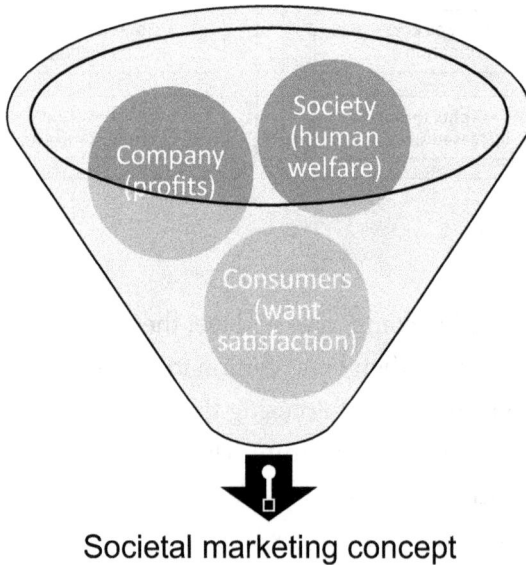

Societal marketing concept

Market Types

In order to satisfy customers, organizations must have an understanding of the market they are competing in. Understanding the market allows organizations to analyze and understand customer needs and wants.

Customer

The customer market refers to customers who buy goods and services for their own use and not for resale. Customer markets are complex because each customer has different likes and dislikes, wants, and needs. Buying habits can differ from customer to customer. There are characteristics that are typically used to distinguish customers from one another. The picture below describes these characteristics.

Figure 1.11

Demographic	Psychographic	Behavioralistic	Geographic
• Gender • Age • Ethnicity • Income • Occupation • Education • Household size • Religion • Generation • Nationality • Social Class	• Interests • Activities • Opinions • Values • Attitudes	• Product usage rates • Brand loyalty • User status • How long have you been a customer? • What benefits is the customer seeking?	• Market size • Region • Population density • Climate

Typically, organizations that are participating in consumer markets spend a lot of time studying consumer behavior. Although we are very interested in what makes a consumer desire and ultimately purchase an item, but we should not stop investigating there. It is important that organizations also understand what satisfies and dissatisfies customers.

Business to Business

The bulk of marketing and sales are from business to business markets. There is more business to business markets because there are several stages that a product goes through starting from the raw material to its end product. Take a textbook for example. First, logs are sold to a business to make the paper. The paper producer sells their paper to a printer. The printer sells their printing services to a publisher. The publisher sells the textbook to a wholesaler. The wholesaler sells the textbook to retail outlets.

How does business to business markets and customer markets differ? Take a look at the diagram below to answer that question.

Figure 1.12

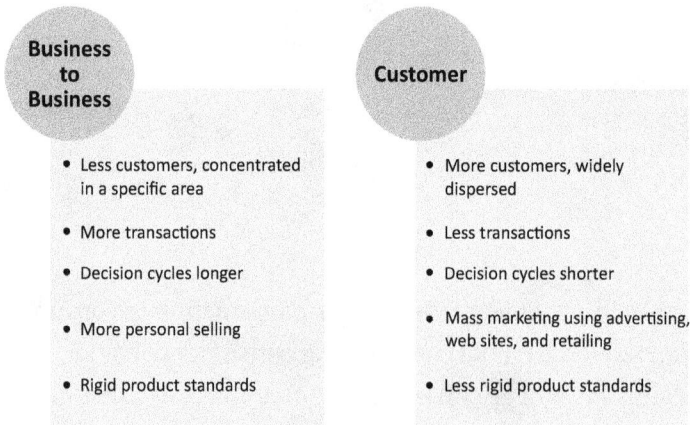

Business to Business
- Less customers, concentrated in a specific area
- More transactions
- Decision cycles longer
- More personal selling
- Rigid product standards

Customer
- More customers, widely dispersed
- Less transactions
- Decision cycles shorter
- Mass marketing using advertising, web sites, and retailing
- Less rigid product standards

Chapter Summary

◆ Market is explained as a group of potential consumers who have a particular need or want in common that are looking for ways to satisfy that need or want through an exchange.

◆ Marketing is defined by the author as a group of processes or procedures for developing, connecting, and providing value to consumers. The main goal of marketing is to fulfill potential consumers' wants, needs, and desires.

◆ Marketing is a critical function completed by an organization to bring greater awareness of the products and services they offer to entice them to purchase them to meet their wants and needs.

◆ Functions of marketing include Customer Relationship Management (CRM), Display, Stockholding, Servicing Risk Taking, Transporting, Market Research, Merchandising, Publicity, Pricing, Forecasting, Buying, Financing, Selling, Public Relations, Sales Promotion.

◆ Stages Of Marketing are Entrepreneurial Marketing, Formulated Marketing, Intrapreneurial Marketing.

◆ Marketing Capacity: What is marketed? Goods, Services, Events, Experiences, Persons, Places, Properties, Organizations, Information, Ideas.

- ◆ Marketing Management is the discipline of selecting goal markets and attaining, possessing and increasing customers through generating, distributing and communicating higher customer value.

- ◆ A marketer's largest responsibility is demand management. Demand Management includes customer management.

- ◆ Types of Markets include Consumer markets, Manufacturer markets, Business Markets, Intermediary Markets, Government Markets.

- ◆ Production Concept: Idea is that consumers will go for products that are available and affordable.

- ◆ Product Concept: Idea is that consumers look for high performance, quality and features.

- ◆ Selling Concept: Idea is that you will never sell enough of a product unless you go for a full-on selling effort.

- ◆ Marketing Concept: Idea is to determine the needs, wants demands of the target market and they must deliver effectively and efficiently.

- ◆ Societal Concept: Same as marketing concept but done in a sustainable way which is beneficial to the consumer's and society's welfare.

- ◆ Market Types include Business to Consumer & Business to Business. Customer Segregation is done on the basis of: Demographic, Psychographic, Behavioristic and Geographical.

Chapter 2

Strategic Planning and Marketing

During planning, organizations also focus on three types of plans:

- **Annual plan** — short term plan describing current state including objectives, strategies, and budgets for the year ahead

- **Long range plan** — overall long-term plan detailing the reasons and factors that the annual plans are structured as they are. This includes forecast for next several years, long term objectives, and main marketing strategies

- **Strategic plan** — overall strategy of how an organization will use its competitive advantages to maintain or attain a successful position in the market. This includes how it fits with overall goals and objectives and the ever-changing environment in the market

All of the elements described above set the stage for the marketing plan, so it is critically important that much research and development go into these elements.

The Process of Planning

When you are working with either the marketing concept or the societal marketing concept, you have to be able to figure out what needs, wants and desires your customer has that are unfulfilled. In order to fulfill this, a series of steps should be followed called the marketing process.

Figure 2.1

Situation Analysis	Marketing Strategy	Marketing Mix Decisions	
• External analysis	• Segmentation	• Product development	**Implementation & Control**
• Internal analysis	• Targeting	• Pricing decisions	
	• Positioning	• Distribution contracts	
	• Value proposition	• Promotional campaign development	

The Strategic Plan

Next, the organization focuses on a statement of their strategy. This statement includes the following elements: strategic intent, mission, vision, and objectives. An organization's strategy statement shapes the organization's long-term strategic path and overall policy directions. With this statement, the organization can outline their map for long term activities.

Strategic intent is part of the strategy statement. This is the reason that the organization is in place today and why it will continue to function in years to come. The strategic intent gives the big picture about an organization that motivates and inspires employees. Priorities are clarified and a clear direction to assist in setting goals and influence resources and core competencies.

Mission

Another piece of the strategy statement is the mission statement. The mission statement is formulated to detail how the organization expects to serve its stakeholders. It gives the "why", "what" and "who" behind an organization. Why is this organization in existence? What does it do or produce? Who does it serve? Mission statements are created to set apart one organization from another. For example, you could say that Wal-Mart and Target are similar stores and therefore have similar answers to the questions above. However, the heart behind what they do and why they do it are completely different. A good mission statement is achievable, clearly stated, motivating, precise, original, investigative, and credible.

In order to create an adequate mission statement, we must be able to answer the following questions:

Figure 2.2

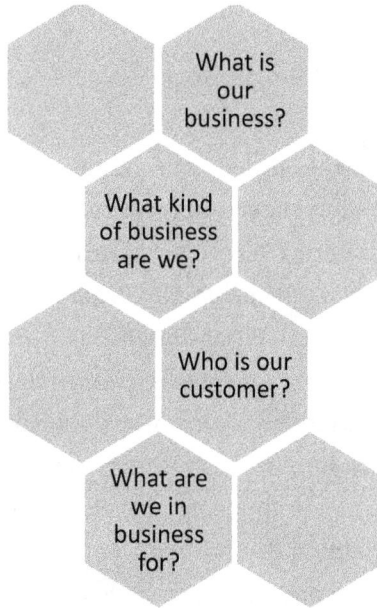

First ask, "What business are we in?" Define in terms not of product or technology, but basic market needs. That way, you are setting up a statement that will withstand the ever-changing technological environment. When you are creating a market-oriented business statement, you describe what conditions need to exist in your business to meet the customer's basic needs.

Next, who is our customer? When defining this question, you can come to several different levels of answers. For example, if we consider an aero-engine company such as Rolls Royce, at one level, we are looking at the airframers. These are the people who launch new aircraft with the Rolls Royce aero-engine. But, who is likely to actually buy the engine? Is it airlines or leasing companies? Who will put pressure on those purchasing to utilize what the aero-engine offers? Pilots, crew, or passengers?

One of the more difficult questions to answer is, "Why are we in business?" This is really difficult for nonprofit organizations to answer such as charities, schools, hospitals, etc. Are they there to educate, train, support, or make healthy? Is the pursuit of knowledge the overarching reason? Really getting down to this answer will definitely drive how you strategize for your organization.

A more strategic directing question is, "What sort of business are we?" Companies may answer this question with things like cost leadership, differentiator, or a focused differentiator.

Vision help to guide the mission, so it is a critical component. This statement is different from the mission statement in that it focuses on where the organization plans to be in the future. Essentially, the vision statement is what the organization wants to be when it grows up. The mission statement go hand in hand. The vision statement describes what the organization will be like if it is successful in achieving its mission. A good vision statement is explicit, clear, in line with organization's cultures and values, realistic, and less lengthy than the mission statement so it can be memorized.

Strategic Objectives

The final component of the strategic statement includes the objectives and goals. A goal is something that an organization is trying to achieve. An objective is a goal we wish to reach over a specified period of time. Goals and objectives break down the mission and vision into more digestible elements. Goals are what we want to reach in order to achieve our mission and vision. Ideal goals and objectives should be exact and measurable, realistic, have defined time frames, address significant issues, and include both financial and non-financial components. Objectives help us to plan how we will meet our goals. Organizations typically have several objectives that can be long term or short term. Objectives are more agile and can change to the environment. Finally, objectives are realistic and operational.

Strategic Audit

The strategic audit includes the internal audit and the external audit. In the external audit, we are looking at the macro environment of a company. The internal audit analyzes all areas of the company and focuses on the value chain as described in Michael Porter's many writings. The sections below seek to detail out these two functions for you to provide better understanding.

Internal Audit

Internal audit of the organizational environment allows you to determine the organization's strengths and weaknesses. By understanding the resources and abilities of your organization, you can identify and capitalize on competitive advantages.

By exploiting the strengths and minimizing exposure of the weaknesses, an organization gains an edge on the competition. The organization has found a way to create value for their consumers. Value is what the consumer is willing to pay for in terms of performance characteristics and attributes. Value is the key to above average returns for an organization. Below is an illustration of how resources, capabilities, core competencies, competitive advantage and strategic competitiveness is interrelated.

Figure 2.3

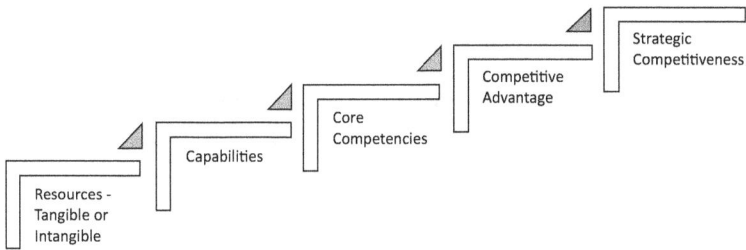

Internal audit is very challenging for managers because the decisions that have to be made are not routine decisions, must be examined ethically, and affect the organization's profitability potential. Before strategic decisions can be made, managers must know what the organization's core competencies are. At the least, the manager should understand the core competencies that are related to going into or leaving new industries, financing new technologies, adding additional manufacturing capacity, and forming strategic relationships.

The challenge in making strategic decisions is that there is a high risk that the company's plans may fail due to interpretation errors. The upside to this is that bad decisions can be corrected if you act quickly and gather the appropriate information to implement the right corrective action. Making these mistakes, can in a sense, be a competitive advantage itself because organizations learn what not to do.

It is helpful to identify the more challenging strategic decisions that need to be made before implementing a plan. Doing this, allows the organization to be very deliberate in data gathering and information interpretation before developing a strategic plan.

Typically, the more challenging strategic decisions have a level of:

- **Uncertainty**   unsure of the qualities of the general and/or industry environments, how competitors may act, and what the consumer prefers

- **Complexity**   causes shaping the environments and viewpoints of the environments are complexly interrelated

- **Interorganizational conflicts**   managers making the decisions and who are affected by these decisions are not in agreement

Decision makers make strategic decisions through learning. They determine if the probability of a certain mistake happening is worth the impact. When a mistake is acknowledged, it is adjusted rapidly, and identification of new possibilities and capabilities occur. Good judgement goes hand in hand with good outcomes in strategic planning. Decision makers may choose to take an educated risk based on the gathered information in decision itself, possible outcomes, possible risks and possible impacts. When good judgement is used, strategic competitiveness is accomplished.

Resources

Resources is one of the key components of competitive advantage. When we bundle resources, we can create a competitive advantage. Resources alone do not generate competitive advantage. At the center of an organization's abilities are resources and they are widespread in scope. This scope can include individual, social and organizational resources. Resources contribute to an organization's production process with two types of resources: tangible and intangible.

Tangible resources can be processed by any of the five senses. Examples of tangible resources can be people, money, or computer hardware. The types of tangible resources you find in an organization are financial, organizational, physical, and technological.

Figure 2.4

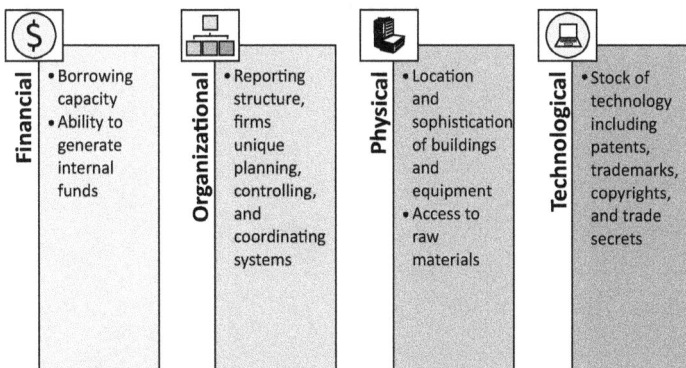

Financial	Organizational	Physical	Technological
• Borrowing capacity • Ability to generate internal funds	• Reporting structure, firms unique planning, controlling, and coordinating systems	• Location and sophistication of buildings and equipment • Access to raw materials	• Stock of technology including patents, trademarks, copyrights, and trade secrets

There are some constraints to the tangible resources. When considering that financial resources can be identified from financial statements, we have to remember that the value of all of the organization's assets is not necessarily reflected in a financial statement. The statement does not take into consideration the intangible resources. Another constraint is that it is challenging to leverage these resources because developing additional business or value from a tangible resource is difficult. For example, you can utilize one team in five different places at the same time. It is also important to remember that some of the processes utilized with tangible assets are intangible. Therefore, it is important to look at resources from both a tangible and intangible viewpoint to ensure you have captured all of your resources.

Intangible resources are typically accumulated over time and are a part of the organization's history. These resources cannot be seen or touched. Examples of intangible resources are knowledge, capabilities of management, trust between leadership and employees, and reputation. There are three types of intangible resources: human, innovation, and reputational.

Figure 2.5

Human	Innovation	Reputation
• Knowledge • Trust • Managerial abilities • Organizational routines	• Ideas • Scientific abilities • Capacity to innovate	• Reputation with customers • Brand name • Consumer viewpoints of product quality, durabilty, and reliability • For efficient, effective, supportive,and mutually beneficial interactions and relationships

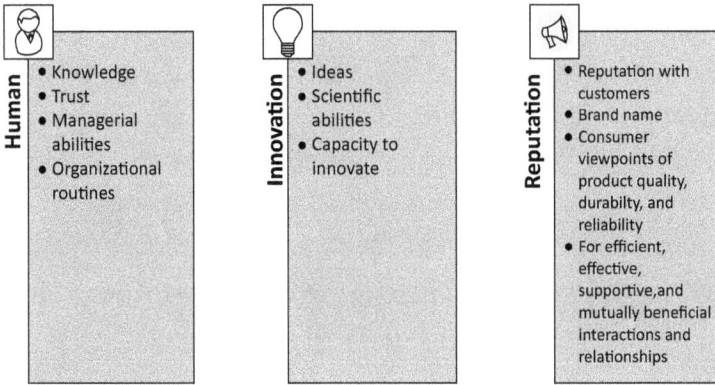

Organizations depend on intangible resources as core competencies because they are not easily discernable and more difficult replicate or substitute for. The more "invisible" a resource is, the better the competitive edge based on it. Intangible resources can be leveraged, unlike tangible resources. Take knowledge for example. People can share knowledge without reducing the value of the resource and in fact, could make the resource even more valuable. Reputation is also an excellent intangible resource. Reputation indicates the level of brand awareness an organization has been able to build amongst its consumers and how highly the consumers think of the organization.

It is generally believed that intangible resources are much more valuable as core competencies than tangible because they are typically what makes an organization unique.

Capabilities

Integrating resources for a specific task or tasks produces capabilities. Building capabilities usually happens over a period of time through complicated activities between intangible and tangible resources. Capabilities frequently come from employee skills and knowledge that is unique to them. Capabilities are also actions that an organization performs remarkably better than competitors. Unique value is added to an organizations products and services through capabilities as well. Typically, you can find capabilities in the following functional areas:

- Distribution

- Human resources

- Information systems

- Marketing

- Management

- Manufacturing

- Research and development

The following table demonstrates some examples of what unique capabilities can emerge from these functional areas.

Table 2.1

Functional Area	Capability
Distribution	Effectively utilizing logistics management policies and procedures
Human resources	Effectively motivating and retaining employees
Information systems	Use of point of purchase data collection methods to effectively and efficiently control inventories
Marketing	Innovative merchandising and advertising
Management	Ability to successfully envision the future of the industry
Manufacturing	Exception product and design quality
Research and development	Ability to quickly transform technology into new products and processes

Core Competencies

Core competencies are the source capabilities of competitive edge an organization has over their competitors. They typically emerge over time and help to differentiate an organization and demonstrate its nature. If we look at all of an organization's resources and capabilities, we will find that only a few of them are strategic assets. Strategic assets are assets that potential sources of competitive advantage and have some sort of competitive value. Some of the assets could prove to be a detriment to the organization because they shine a light on areas that the organization is weaker in. There isn't a magic number of core competencies that an organization is required to have in order to have the competitive advantage. However, most effective strategic plans can be built around three to four competencies. There is caution in having too many core competencies because organizations tend to lose their focus on the core competencies that can really give them the upper hand over competitors.

When recognizing and developing core competencies, organizations usually use the standards for a supportable advantage and/or value chain analysis. When we are determining our competitive advantage, we want to make sure that it is something that can be maintained and lost easily. Using the criteria of usefulness, uniqueness, expensive replication, and no viable alternatives helps us to decide can we afford to maintain this advantage? Does it make sense? The value chain analysis allows organizations to determine which core competencies should be invested in to be maintained since they are creating value for consumers. The value chain also helps us to map out the process, so we can understand what areas might benefit from being outsourced.

Figure 2.6

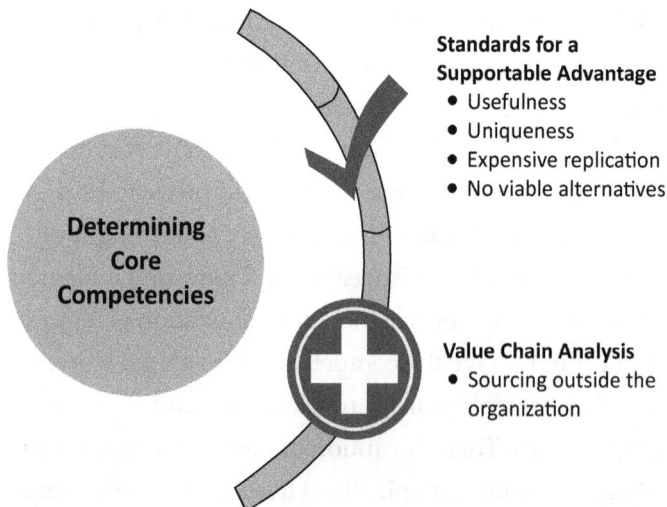

**Standards for a
Supportable Advantage**
- Usefulness
- Uniqueness
- Expensive replication
- No viable alternatives

**Determining
Core
Competencies**

Value Chain Analysis
- Sourcing outside the
  organization

Standards for a Supportable Advantage

Core competencies should meet these four criteria:

- **Usefulness** how useful is it and does it have real value? Can it be used to reduce threats and create opportunities?

- **Uniqueness** specific to an organization itself, no other organization owns it

- **Expensive replication** is the cost of replicating the product too high to make it worth it?

- **No viable alternatives** there are no alternatives out there that can take its place

Capabilities that do not meet the four criteria are not core competencies. The table below gives you a better idea of what happens when all criteria are not met.

Table 2.2

Is it useful enough to present a threat to competitors?	Is it unique enough to give us a competitive advantage?	Is the cost of replicating the product too high to be worth it?	Are there any other alternative solutions out there?	Is there a competitive advantage?	Is there a competitive disadvantage?	What does performance look like?
No	No	No	No		✓	Less than average
Yes	No	No	Yes/no	Competitive parity		Average
Yes	Yes	No	Yes/no	✓ But temporary		Average and possibly slightly above average
Yes	Yes	Yes	Yes	✓		Above average

Value Chain

The ability to be able to identify areas of operation that do and do not add value is referred to as the value chain analysis. This is an important piece to understand because an organization's profit potential increases when the value they create is more than the costs they incur. The value chain is a template that is used by organizations to clarify their cost position and direct the implementation of a specific business-level strategy through primary and support activities. Primary activities in the value chain bring the product to the consumer. These activities would include creating the product itself, selling and shipping it to buyers, and providing customer service after the sale. Support activities are assistance activities that occur to make sure that the primary activities happen. The most valuable piece in the value chain as a whole are people who have the knowledge of their consumers.

Let's look at the primary activities in the value chain a little closer. Below are the primary activities defined:

- **Inbound logistics** actions that are utilized to receive, store, and distribute inputs to a product

- **Operations** actions that convert the inputs into the final product

- **Outbound logistics** actions that include gathering, storing, and shipping out the product to consumers

- **Marketing and sales** actions to entice consumers to purchase the product and providing outlets for the consumers to purchase from

- **Service**   action that boost or preserve the value of the product

Figure 2.7

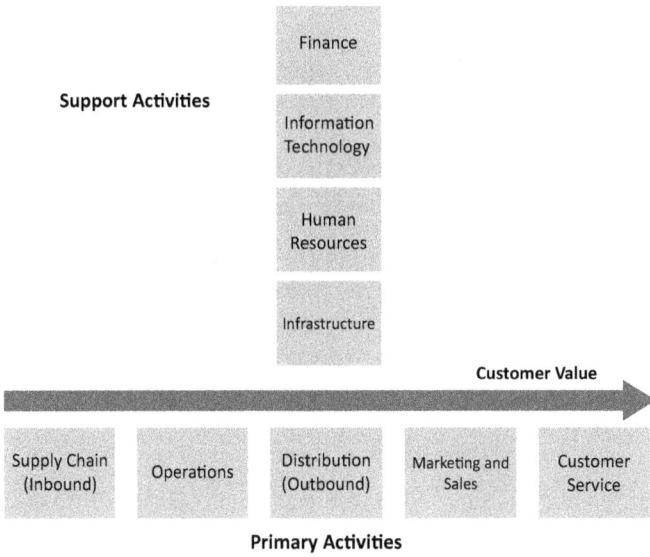

Figure 2.8

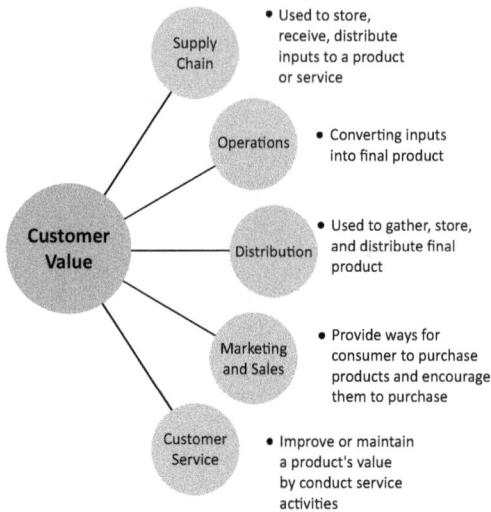

Value Chain - Primary Activities

Using the Value Chain

The first step in using the value chain is to identify the primary activities of the value chain for your organization. The next step is to identify sub activities for each primary activity that helps to create value. There are different types of sub activities:

- **Direct**　　creates value by itself

- **Indirect**　　assists direct activities in running easily

- **Quality assurance**　　helps to make sure that both direct and indirect activities are meeting standards of quality

Next, ask the question, what are the activities that fall under of the support activities? Out of all of the primary activity sub activities, which ones generate the most value? Essentially, you are following the lower level activities through the value chain and detailing what the value add is and if it is significant. After these step, determine if the sub activities are direct, indirect, or apply to quality assurance. Are there other activities that are value adding that are part of your organization's infrastructure? If so, capture those as well. They may not be related directly to a primary activity and you will also want to determine if they are direct, indirect, or related to quality assurance.

Fourth, ask the question, "How are all of these activities related?" Once you begin to answer this question, you begin to piece together your organization's competitive advantage from a value-chain viewpoint. For example, there is a link between sales force training and sales volumes.

Finally, ask yourself the question, "How can I improve or maximize the value my organization gives to the consumer with our products and services?"

Figure 2.9

Value Chain – Support Activities

A few important things to remember when identifying your organization's value chain:

- Align proposed changes with your organization's overall business strategies.

- Determine a process and prioritize your list.

- This process gives you a big picture perspective. For a more in-depth look, conduct a value chain analysis.

Value Chain Analysis

A value chain analysis includes three steps:

- **Activity analysis**   what activities do you complete to provide your service?

- **Value analysis**   what can your organization add to these activities to provide the highest value to the consumer?

- **Evaluation and planning**   examine the list of things you developed from point b) above and determine if completing the change would add enough value to be worth the work

The activity analysis step includes brainstorming with your team or organization to list all the actions you take that add value or enhance your consumer's experience. Taking this from a top-down approach, you can first consider what this looks like from an organization level. An example of actions that the organization takes that adds value is the defined business process that are used to provide service to the consumer. These actions an include marketing, operations procedures, distribution, and customer support. If you look at this from an individual or team level, the actions would be the ones you do on a day to day basis that carry out the work you do. Also, be sure to include everything that adds value, not just the obvious daily activities to provide the product. For example, activities like motivating team members, recruiting a skilled workforce, or research and development on the latest technologies.

An important thing to remember about this brainstorming activity is that you will get more ideas and better answers if you brainstorm with a team rather than just brainstorming by yourself. Also, going through the exercise and coming up with ideas will encourage better buy in from team members regarding the proposed changes you come up with out of the exercise.

After you have generated your list of activities from brainstorming, identify correlating "Value Factors" with each item. Value factors are things that your consumers place value on due to the method each activity is completed. Let's look at a doctor's office for example. One of the things on your list may be the nurse call process. Your consumer probably puts a high value on how quickly the nurse answers the phone or calls them back, how polite they are, and how knowledgeable they are. After you have identified the value of each activity in your list, examine what could be modified to give an even greater value to the consumer.

The last step is to look at the modifications you have listed and develop a plan for the next steps to be taken. The previous step will result in a long list of activities that would be great if you could complete all of them. It is important to take a moment and think through how you will complete the changes you have listed and accomplish what you set out for in a timely manner. Instead of going down the list in the order in which you listed them, take time to prioritize. Pick the low hanging fruit first. These activities are ones that are easy and quick to complete. Look through the remainder of the list and ask, "Is this change worth it?" and "what does the real value add at the end of the day?" Remove items from the list that require a large work effort and little value add. Then, prioritize the rest of your list in a way that will allow a steady pace of achievement and add value to keep both team members and consumers excited about your organization's products and solutions. Another option for assistance in prioritizing the list is to consult with a customer you work closely with to get their input on the list regarding what would be most valuable.

Outsourcing

When an organization purchases a value adding activity from a supplier that is external, they are outsourcing. Outsourcing allows organizations to be more flexible, alleviate risks, and decrease their investments in capital. More organizations are turning to outsourcing because they cannot obtain the resources and capabilities necessary to reach a competitive advantage in every primary and support activity. Outsourcing allows organizations to focus on the core competencies they really excel at.

If you intend to get involved in outsourcing at your organization, it is critical that you have the following skillsets: tactical thinking, negotiating, partnership authority, and change management. You need to be a strategic thinker because you must understand your organization's core competencies and how an outsourcing partner could help your competitive edge. You must be able to make deals or negotiate with outsourcers, so they can be used by organization management. You should be empowered to oversee and manage the relationship with the outsourcer. Finally, utilizing outsourcing can require a large amount of change so it is very important that you are able to manage change.

The biggest downfall of outsourcing is the growing concerns from communities regarding the loss of jobs for local workers to outsourced companies. There is also a possible risk of loss capability to effectively innovate. When considering outsourcing at your organization, you should be sure to plan for these concerns from consumers and employees and be ready to discuss it.

There are also advantages to outsourcing. It can possibly decrease costs and improve the quality of the actions that have been outsourced. By doing this, you add value to the products and services you provide to the customer. Therefore, outsourcing can result in a competitive advantage for an organization and allow value to be created for its stakeholders.

Case Study

Let's look at Apple as a case study for determine strengths and weaknesses. Apple is a household name. Most consumers have heard of Apple the company are aware of some of items they produce such as the iPhone. This awareness is called brand awareness and it is probably one of the biggest strengths of Apple. They also have a strong brand identity. Consumers may describe their products as aesthetically pleasing and creative. The Apple brand can also be described as a status symbol. iPhones are coveted by consumers because they associate them with an extravagant or wealthy lifestyle. They are willing to wait for hours on end just to obtain the newest version of the phone.

What are Apple's weaknesses? First, their products are costly which definitely eliminates some consumers. The population who can afford their products are narrowed by their price point. The high price of their product is part of the prestige that is a strength, but it does affect them negatively by limiting the number of consumers that can purchase their product.

Business Portfolio

When we refer to the business portfolio, we are describing all of the businesses and products that are a part of our company. This is the key to the relationship between the strategy and its individual parts of the business. Your goal in creating your business portfolio is to create one that fits with the organization's strengths and weaknesses as well as considering the opportunities that are readily available in the environment. When "working" the business portfolio, the organization is examining or analyzing which areas deserve the most attention and investment and determining how to create strategies where developing new products or businesses grows the organization.

The first step is to analyze the business portfolio. In analysis, leadership takes a close look at all of the businesses in the organization and evaluates them to determine where resources should and should not go. What are the key items that make up the company? Perhaps you want to invest the most resources in those items. These key units are also referred to as strategic business units (SBUs). SBUs are defined as separate entities in an organization that have their own mission and objectives. They can be treated as an independent unit from the other organization businesses. Examples of an SBU are an organization division, product line, or a brand. The next step after analysis is to look at the SBUs and determine which ones deserve more attention and resources. A great way to do this is to use the Boston Consulting Group box shown below.

Figure 2.10

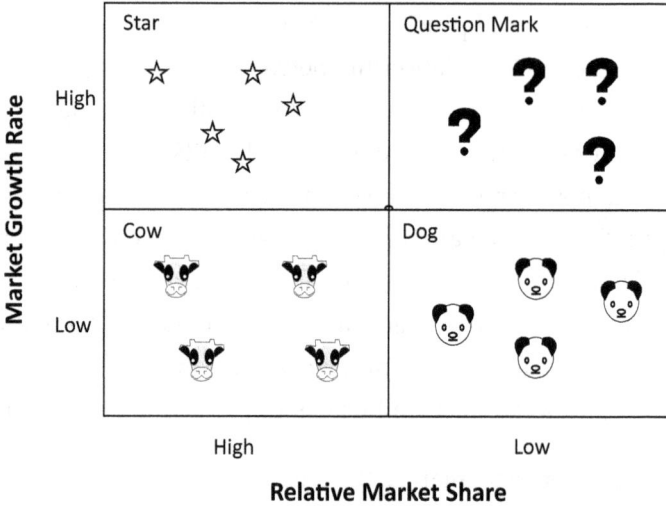

The diagram above is referred to as a growth-share matrix. When you are looking at the axes, you see that the vertical axis refers to market share while the horizontal axis refers to the growth rate. In essence, this diagram uses market attractiveness and the company strength to classify strategic business units. When you do this, you can break down the SBUs into four different categories.

- **Stars**   Populating the high growth rate and high relative market share section of this diagram are stars. Stars usually require significant investment to keep them growing quickly. After a while, these SBUs will slowdown in growth rate and become cash cows.

- **Cash cows**   The growth rate is low, but the market share is high for cash cows. Since they are not growing as rapidly as other SBUs, they do not require as significant an investment. Cash cows keep the lights on and the bills paid from the revenue they generate on a consistent basis.

- **Question marks**   High growth rates with low market share result in question marks. You need investment for these SBUs to be maintained much less grow them. Question marks require managers to question whether to put in the investment for these items to grow or if they should be discontinued.

- **Dogs**   Low growth and low market share SBUs are referred to as dogs. These SBUs can sustain themselves but do not generate any additional revenue for the company.

After an organization determines what their SBUs can be classified as, they must determine how they will be utilized in the future. Is the question mark worth the investment? Is the star still growing or is it time for it to be phased into a cash cow? Strategic decision making depending upon these classifications is crucial to maintain and grow market share. This classification can also be used to forecast the life cycle of an SBU. Many of the SBUs start out as question marks and, with significant investment, become stars. As the growth rate begins to decrease, the SBU becomes a cash cow. Since cash cows generate income and require a lesser investment, it is critical to always be looking for SBUs that can be turned into cash cows from stars. Organizations want to continuously be developing SBUs to go through this cycle to sustain operations.

Another way to plan your business portfolio is to use the General Electric grid. They refer to it as a strategic-planning grid. In this grid, business strength is on the horizontal axis while industry attractiveness resides on the vertical axis.

Figure 2.11

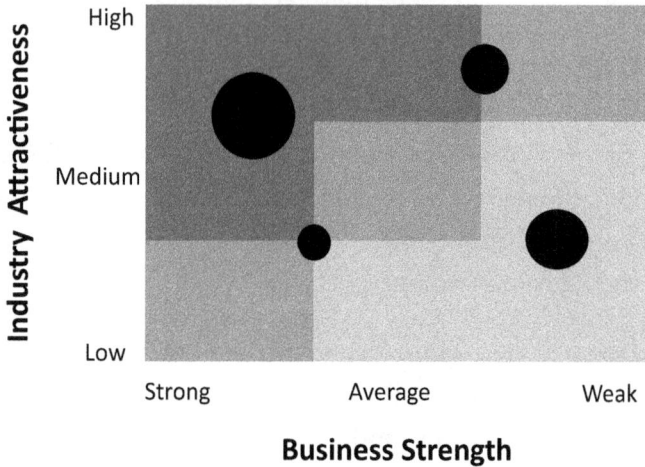

Business Strength

This grid looks at several things as a part of industry attractiveness including market size, growth rate, profit margin in the industry, level of competition, demand cycle, and structure of cost in the industry. All of these items are considered as a part of industry attractiveness. In the diagram example above, we are rating attractiveness as high medium or low.

Instead of simply using market share, the GE grid uses an index for business strength just like it does with industry attractiveness. Items that factor into business strength can include organization market share, competitiveness of price, quality of the good or service, customer and market familiarity, sales success and advantages in the geography. Usually these factors are all taken into consideration and then categorized into strong, average or weak.

The grid is further divided into three areas. The blue area represents strong SBUs that should be invested in, so they can grow and flourish. The orange area shows SBUs that come in at a medium level of attractiveness and therefore should be maintained with investment. The purple area includes SBUs that are overall week and low in attractiveness. Careful consideration should be given to whether to discontinue or harvest these SBUs.

The circles in the diagram represent the SBUs and the size relates to the size of the industries they are in. You can take these circles a step further and divide them into pie slices to represent market share of the SBU. The same idea of strategic planning with the previous diagram also applies to this diagram. The idea is to look at the SBUs in the diagram, make strategic decisions about their future which will help to grow and sustain the organization, and determine where new growth needs to occur when forecasting how an SBU will cycle through the grid. With this grid, managers can plot current state and future state to help them decided where some issues may arise and where the opportunities are.

Both of the tools mentioned above, although are very helpful with strategic planning, have their flaws. Developing the grids themselves is time consuming. Implementing the changes determined from the grid can be costly. Definition of SBUS, their market share, and growth can sometimes be challenging to define. These approaches also place a lot of emphasis on current state with no advice for planning for the future. Also, using these approaches can cause organizations to place greater emphasis on the items that categorize the SBUs, which can lead to loss of awareness of other elements that may affect overall strategic planning.

External Audit

The external analysis of the organizational environment allows you to determine the organization's opportunities and threats. Opportunities are described as an opportunity to exploit an external condition that will improve the organization's strategic competitiveness. A threat is just the opposite. A threat is a condition in the general environment that could detrimentally affect an organization's strategic competitiveness.

When you are completing an external analysis, you are collecting and analyzing data on the industry, national environment, and the socio-economic environment. During this analysis, we are concerned about the competitors in the industry and their position as well as our position in the industry. We are also looking at how the environment as a whole could affect us and our long-term planning including economic, social, governmental, legal, technological, national and international factors.

Let's continue with the Apple case study and look at their external factors. An opportunity externally that Apple has demonstrated time and time again is their unique ability to be able to effectively and efficiently collaborate with other companies. They have collaborated with companies that produce popular headphones to create a wireless Airpod product. They have also worked with gaming companies to have games specially created for the iPhone. On the flip side of opportunities, are threats. A huge threat that Apple faces is the large amount of imitation that occurs in the marketplace. Companies produce products that are similar to Apple products and a lower price point. Competition is also a big threat for Apple. Companies like Samsung advertise that their products have just as much functionality, if not more, at a lower price point, with less hassle and cost of future upgrades.

Environments - General

When completing an external analysis, you should consider three environments:

- General

- Industry

- Competitor

The general environment is described as broader societal dimensions that influence an industry its organizations. These dimensions are divided into seven segments including:

- Demographic

- Economic

- Political/Legal

- Sociocultural

- Technological

- Global

- Physical

Please refer to the table below for more detail on the elements included in these dimensions. In order to create successful strategic plan, organizations should be knowledgeable of these dimensions.

- **Demographic**

  - Population size

  - Age structure

  - Geographic distribution

  - Ethnic mix

  - Income distribution

- **Economic**

  - Inflation

  - Interest rates

  - Trade deficits or surpluses

  - Personal savings rate

  - Business savings rates

  - Gross domestic product (GDP)

- **Political/Legal Antitrust laws**

  - Taxation laws

  - Deregulation philosophies

  - Labor training laws

  - Educational philosophies and policies

- **Sociocultural Women in the workforce**

  - Women in the workforce

  - Attitudes about quality

  - Concerns about the environment

- Shifts in work and career preferences
- Shifts in preferences regarding product and service characteristics

- **Technological**

  - Product innovations
  - Applications of knowledge
  - Focus of private and government-supported R&D expenditures
  - New communication technologies

- **Global**

  - Important political events
  - Critical global markets
  - Newly industrialized countries
  - Different cultural and institutional attributes

- **Physical**

  - Energy consumption
  - Practices used to develop energy sources
  - Renewable energy efforts
  - Minimizing an organization's environmental footprint
  - Availability of water as a resource
  - Producing environmentally friendly products
  - Reacting to natural or man-made disasters

It is important to note that the general environment cannot be controlled by organizations. Therefore, companies that are successful in this environment have a deep understanding of the segments, gather the appropriate data and analyze it, and then account for what they find in their strategies. Organizations are influenced by the current states of the segments.

When organizations study the demographic segments, they try to consider the global climate due to possible effects in different countries since organizations may compete in global markets. When analyzing the economic segment, we are considering the where the economy is now and where it is going. Examining this segment helps to plan to meet a general goal of most organizations which is to compete in an industry that is relatively stable with potential for growth. The political/legal segment learn about the relationships between organizations and the government. We look at how they impact each other in the current state and how future state might be impacted so we can plan accordingly. Society's values, attitudes, and cultural views are considered in the sociocultural segment. These things can actually affect how the demographic, economic, political/legal, and technological segments behave and evolve. Innovation with new products, processes, and resources is the focal point of the technological segment. This segment includes developing new learnings and converting that knowledge into products, services, resources, and processes. The global segment looks at new and current markets, how they are changing, pertinent international events, and critical cultural qualities. Finally, the physical segment is focusing on supporting the environment. Organizations have begun to gain a clearer understanding of how the physical environment can influence business practices, so they include this segment to plan accordingly.

The industry environment that organizations refer to can consist of things like demographics, shifts in lifestyle and economic cycles per businessdictionary.com. It includes Porter's Five Forces: risk of new competitors, power of suppliers and buyers, risk of duplication, and intensity of competitor rivalry. The key to this environment is to find a position in the market where your organization can positively influence the forces or successfully protect themselves against their influence. This is particularly helpful in volatile industries like the airline industry where there is intense rivalry amongst competitors and getting pushed out of the industry is relatively common even for the industry's leaders.

Gathering information about other competitors in the industry and analyzing that data is referred to as competitor analysis and is used to understand the competitive environment. Competitor analysis couple with the information from industry and general environment analysis give organizations a great big picture of what they are dealing with. General environment analysis focuses on forecasting the future. Industry environment analysis is pinpoints the influences on an organization's profitability potential within its industry. Looking at analysis on competitors helps us understand how competitors may act in the future so that your organization can respond appropriately.

In an effort to better manage and comprehend the current environment, organizations conduct external environmental analysis. This analysis is comprised of four segments: scanning, monitoring, forecasting, and assessing.

Figure 2.12

Scanning	• What changes or trends in the environment raise a red flag?
Monitoring	• After ongoing observation, what changes or trends in the environment raise a red flag?
Forecasting	• What do we think can happen as a result of the changes and trends we have been observing?
Assessing	• What is the timing and criticality of these changes or trends in the environment?How can we include them in future strategies?

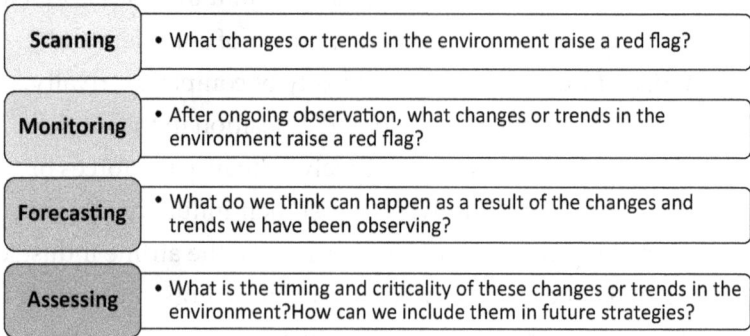

There are many sources that can be referenced when you are collecting data on the general environment. Those sources include:

- Trade publications
- Newspapers
- Business publications
- Academic research
- Public polls
- Trade shows
- Suppliers
- Customers
- Employees

Scanning

The first step in the external environmental analysis process is scanning. Scanning involves looking at all segments in the general environment. Scanning often results in early signals of possible changes and helps to identify any changes that are already happening. This part of the process is a data gathering activity. You collect raw data from several different sources but how the information is related is still unclear and often incomplete. It is important that the scanning activities are in alignment with the environment. For example, the scanning system for a stable environment should be calibrated for stable environments not volatile environments.

Today, organizations often utilize software specialized to identify these changes and trends. This software is set up to look for specific pieces of information which can sometimes cause a false alarm. Organizations are willing to take the tradeoff of this software raise false alarms if it increases the probability of early detection of red flags. Another way to detect changes is by using capabilities in internet browsers that allows organizations to collection information about those who click through their sight.

Monitoring

At this step, researchers are sifting through the data gathered to determine what pieces are meaningful. After determining this, they begin to actively monitor the changes and trends to see if something worthwhile that could affect their strategies is happening in the environment. To be effective in monitoring, organizations must accurately identify their stakeholders and know what their standing is amongst those stakeholders.

Understanding this allows organizations to meet the needs of their unique population they serve. Industries with high technological ambiguity find scanning and monitoring particularly critical. It gives them information, develops new knowledgebase items about the environment, and helps them determine the best strategies for marketing their new technologies.

Forecasting

After monitoring the trends and performance of the current environment, analysts gather the information and use it to help them determine what could happen in the future and when. For example, analysts may forecast how long it will take the government to put a particular regulation in place or how quickly a competitor is bringing a new technology to the consumer. Technology is improving at such a rapid rate, that it often expedites the product life cycle which, in turn, makes accurate forecasting difficult. Therefore, the greatest challenge in forecasting is accuracy. If you are unable to forecast close to accurate, your potential profitability could be affected. For example, Company A forecasted a 22% increase in sales for 2017 but the increase was actually 32%. Your first reaction may be positive since we sold even more than we had anticipated. But, the supplies for your products were ordered in quantity to support a 22% increase in sales. Company A found itself in a situation where they had more demand than supply due to not estimating for the larger increase. This did affect profitability because the company was unable to sell as much as what the customer was demanding.

Assessing

We have collected the data, pieced it together and determined what pieces are meaningful and what is not. Now, understanding the timing and significance of the effects of the changes and trends on strategic management is important. The organization is now postulating the effects of the things they have learned on the organization itself. The key thing to remember here is that how the data is interpreted is paramount. If the interpretation of the information gathered is incorrect, inadequate strategies are developed and the organization profitability is affected. Many companies gather the data and organize but they do not assess it to see what it means to them. In these cases, they are increasing their risk of an inaccurate strategy implementation. Assessing ensures that the proposed strategy is correct.

Environments – Competitive

After completing an industry analysis described in an earlier chapter, the last piece of external analysis is a competitor analysis. In this analysis we are looking at every company that your organization competes with. This analysis is most interested in the competitor's objectives, strategies, assumptions, and abilities. In this analysis, we want to know:

- **The competitor's driving force** what objectives do they want to reach in the long term?

- **The competitor's current state** what are their current strategic plans?

- **The competitor's industry beliefs** what do they

believe to be true regarding the industry?

- **The competitor's abilities**   where is the organization strong and where is the organization weak?

Having this information allows an organization to determine how to respond.

Figure 2.13

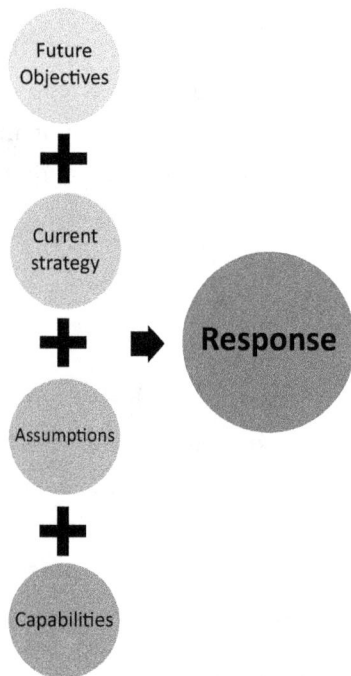

When an organization considers future objectives, they are looking at:

- In comparison to our competitors, what do our goals look like?

- In the future, where should we place the most importance?

- How risk averse are we?

When an organization considers current strategy, they are looking at:

- Currently, how are we competing?

- Are changes in the competitive structure supported in their strategies?

When an organization considers assumptions, they are looking at:

- Are we assuming a volatile or stable future?

- Is status quo how we are functioning?

- What are the assumptions that our competitors hold when they look at the industry and themselves?

When an organization looks at capabilities they are looking at:

- Where are we strong and weak?

- If we were to rate us and our competitors, where do we fall in the list?

Using the answers to these questions we can determine a response that answers the following questions:

- Our competitors are likely to do (fill in the blank) in the future.

- What do we have to offer over our competitors?

- Does this change our relationship with our competitors? How?

Case Study

Let's take a case study of a successful environmental scanning example and an unsuccessful environmental scanning example.

PepsiCo

PepsiCo, popular soft drink and beverage manufacturer completed an environmental scan and found that health and wellness is becoming a big part of the food and beverage industry today as well as other industries. The CEO took this to heart and began developing a long-term strategy to include health snacks and beverage alternatives in their portfolio of products. The CEO has a goal of tripling their healthy products business by the year 2020. The company decided to use an acquisition strategy to get them into the health and wellness market more quickly with already successful products such as those manufactured by Naked. They also have increased the research and development budget related to healthier ingredients that can be backward engineered into their current products.

PepsiCo made the right decision at the right time to move with the industry quickly. Other companies have suffered because they did not do appropriate planning to incorporate health and wellness.

Borders

Borders filed for bankruptcy in 2011 due to poor environmental scanning and not acting on what was returned from environmental scanning analysis. Despite reports of a growing internet presences from other stores in the industry and an increased use of online purchasing outlets, Borders chose to invest in its CD business and its physical book business instead of focusing on beefing up their internet presence. Environmental scanning also indicated that digital downloads were on the up rise for CDs as well as eBooks for books. Due to their lack of reaction to these environmental trends, they were forced out of business. This is definitely an example of poor management of environmental scanning and its analysis.

The Marketing Plan

Each strategy plan has a marketing plan for each business or SBU. Since products can widely differ, it is very important to have different marketing plans for each item.

A typical marketing plan holds many elements. The following picture shows the elements that make up the marketing plan.

Figure 2.14

Executive Summary	Current Marketing State	SWOT Analysis
Marketing Strategy	Action plans	Budgets
	Controls	

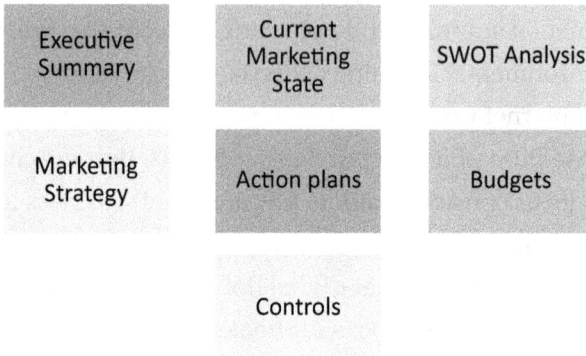

Marketing Plan Elements

The executive summary is a short summary of what you will find in the detailed marketing plan. This includes what the main goals of the plan are and any important recommendations you wish to include. When developing this summary, ask yourself, "what are the quick points I want chief executives to know if they just glance at this plan?" A template for this summary may be used below to help guide your summary development.

Marketing plan name: (include product name in plan name)

Goals and objectives:

- Goal

- Goal

- Goal

Risks:

- Risk

- Risk

- Risk

Recommendations:

- Recommendation

- Recommendation

- Recommendation

The marketing current state describes the current situation and background. It may include market, product, competition and distribution data. The current state includes in your internal and external audits described in earlier sections of this document. Using this information, you are able to thoroughly examine your organization's internal and external environments to locate possible problem areas and opportunities. The beginning of the report should describe the focus market and the organization's current position in it. The report should be driven from the perspective of the strategic imperatives including objectives, policies and strategies passed down from other plans. The next area of the report focuses on current state. In current state we look at market information and details (also known as market description), how the product performs, competitors, and dissemination. Next, product review details the sales, prices and gross margins of the top products in the line. After that, the competition section describes top competitors and strategies for quality, pricing, dissemination, and marketing. Lastly, the distribution section maps out recent sales trends in the main distribution channels.

Figure 2.15

Market
Description

Product Review

Competition

Distribution

The SWOT analysis pulls strengths, weaknesses, threats, and opportunities from the current market state. It shows a list of factors that are critical to success as well. SWOT diagrams can help you decide whether a business venture or new product is worth moving forward with. It also serves as a great picture for how to allocate resources and plan for future marketing efforts.

SWOT analysis are completed by going through the following steps:

- State your objective

- Develop a grid

- Label each area, "Strengths", "Weaknesses", "Opportunities", and "Threats"

- Add appropriate strengths and weaknesses both qualitative and quantitative

- Conclude

Figure 2.16

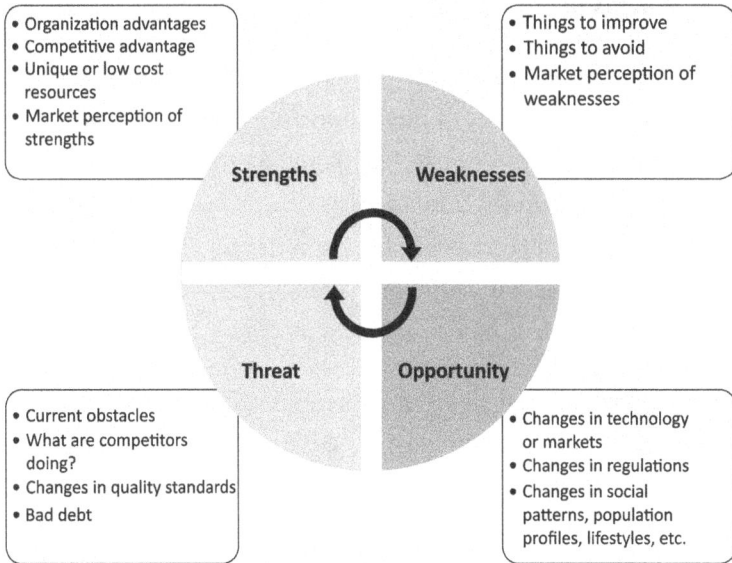

- Organization advantages
- Competitive advantage
- Unique or low cost resources
- Market perception of strengths

Strengths

- Things to improve
- Things to avoid
- Market perception of weaknesses

Weaknesses

Threat

- Current obstacles
- What are competitors doing?
- Changes in quality standards
- Bad debt

Opportunity

- Changes in technology or markets
- Changes in regulations
- Changes in social patterns, population profiles, lifestyles, etc.

In the marketing strategy section of the marketing plan, we look at the overall strategy or plan of attack meeting the goals. Basically, this section outlines how you plan to achieve marketing goals. This section segments the market into digestible pieces, so you can easily address how each segment will be handled to meet strategic objectives.

The action plans tell you what will happen when "the rubber meets the road." This plan answers critical questions about the marketing strategy:

- What will we do?

- When will we do it?

- Who will do it?

- What is the cost?

The plan details when actions will be started and finished. Project profit and loss with the supporting marketing budget. The budget looks at forecasted sales and average price for revenues. For expenses, it includes production, dissemination, and marketing. The difference between the two is the projected profit. This budget will assist managers in their purchases and actions moving forward.

Control is the final element to the marketing plan. It essentially details how the process will be controlled and monitored for progress. This section helps us tell upper level management how we measure up to the goals and objectives we set with the marketing plan. Marketing control is the method of quantifying and appraising the outcomes of marketing tactics and plans and making changes to ensure that the marketing objectives are achieved. In order to properly measure and document marketing controls, we must answer the following questions:

- What is the goal?

- What is occurring?

- Why is it occurring?

- What should our next step be?

Answering these questions allows us to establish goals, measure how we perform to those goals, evaluate how we are performing, and determine if any corrective action needs to be taken.

Figure 2.17

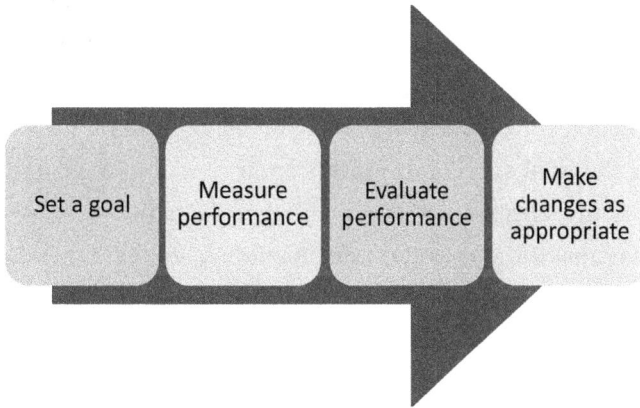

Implementation

The marketing plan is only as good as how effectively it is implemented. Marketing implementation can be described as the process of creating marketing actions out of marketing strategies to facilitate achieving objectives.

In order for implementation to be successful, it is critically important that all employees at all levels of the organization are dedicated to implementing the plan. Marketing strategies are broken down to actions at a day to day task level that must be consistently implemented. Successful implementations are also a product of an organization's ability to effectively blend its people, structure, decision procedures, reward mechanisms, and culture into one cohesive program that supports the strategy well. Decision procedures and reward mechanisms can also be a deciding factor of success. If leaders are incented to meet budget or show short term results, the likelihood of success increases as the manager works to attain the incentive. Finally, marketing strategy must be hand in hand with the organization's culture. The culture guides the employee's actions on every level and if the two are well fitted, strategy becomes easier to achieve.

Chapter Summary

◆ The three types of plans are Annual (short term), Long range (long-term), and Strategic (competitive advantage).

◆ The marketing process consists of a situational analysis, marketing strategy, marketing mix decision making, and implementation/control.

◆ Strategic Audit contains an internal and external audit process.

◆ Internal audits: determine an organization's strengths and weaknesses

◆ Organization's Resources include Tangible resources and Intangible resources.

◆ Value can be added to any product and services through capabilities, such as distribution, human resources, information systems, marketing, management, manufacturing and R&D.

◆ Core competencies are the source capabilities that are useful, unique, require expensive replication and have no viable alternatives, and what organizations have over their competitors.

◆ A Value Chain identifies an organization's cost position based on primary and support activities, and includes Inbound Logistics, Operations, Outbound logistics, Marketing and Sales, and Services.

This page is intentionally left blank

Chapter 3

Research in Marketing

I n order to carry out all of the work described in the previous sections, research must be completed to gather all of the information needed. This information is referred to as market research. In the next sections we will discuss how to pull together the information and interpret it.

Information Systems

Information systems exist for almost every business function. The same is true for marketing. A Marketing Information System (MIS) uses people, equipment, and procedures to pull together, organize, review, interpret, and disseminate marketing information to the appropriate decision makers. Marketing managers are the operators, in a sense, of the MIS. First, the marketing manager works with the MIS to determine the marketing question(s)that needs an answer. Next, the MIS pulls from various information sources to construct the needed information for the marketing manager. Lastly, the MIS distributes the gathered information to the manager to help answer the posed question(s), so they can plan, implement, and control operations moving forward. The marketing manager walks hand in hand with the MIS throughout the entire process.

Figure 3.1

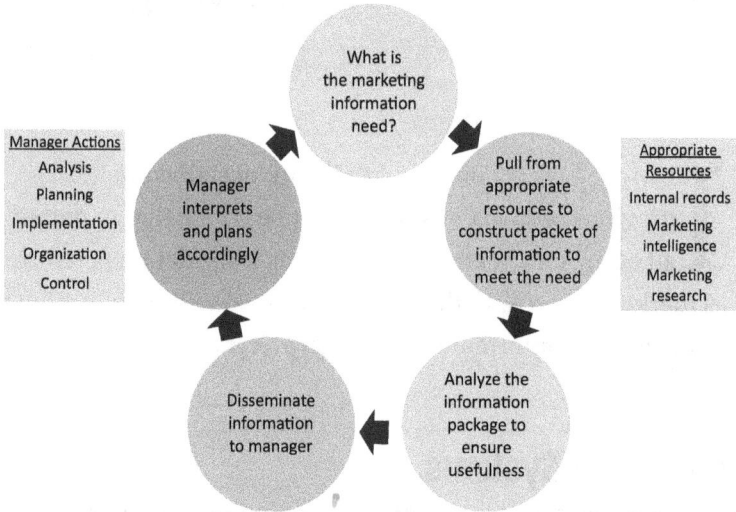

Constructing Information

Information is constructed from various resources. These resources can be classified into three different categories including internal records, marketing intelligence, and marketing research. The information system pulls this information and packages it together to ensure that the information is presented in the correct context, is appropriate, and applicable to the marketing question at hand.

If we examine further, we can describe internal records as information that is gathered internally from the organization to help identify strengths and weakness, issues and opportunities, and overall performance. This information could include things such as financial statements, sales records, reporting on manufacturing efficiencies and capabilities, and customer service feedback and issues. Utilizing internal records is a quick function and is low cost as compared to trying to pull information from outside sources. The downside is that the information can often be incomplete or not in a context or format that is useful for marketing purposes. An even larger problem is the sheer amounts of data and information a company can generate. The effort of combing through this information for the right data can be time consuming and difficult to find or track.

Marketing and Competitor Intelligence

Another area is marketing intelligence. Marketing intelligence is described as information about the current marketing environment and its developments that can help managers create and manage their marketing plans. This intelligence is gathered by scouring the current environment and delivering it to the marketing manager. Often marketing intelligence comes from the organization's own employees. They are a great source of information but can be difficult to pull the information out of because they do not understand the importance of the base of knowledge they have. Marketing managers use persuasion to get buy in from employees to encourage their participation buy thorough explaining the importance of communicating what they know. Other source of marketing intelligence can be suppliers and customers. Persuasion is also needed to encourage these groups to provide information. Information can often be pulled from public sources about competitors because competitors report it out themselves. These public sources can include annual reports, advertisements, and reports in the press. Finally, information can be bought from outside suppliers. There are several research companies available out there that will sell marketing intelligence to companies when requested.

Marketing intelligence refers to the marketing environment in general whereas competitor intelligence is information collected that specifically focuses on the competitor and what they are doing. Some organizations spend extensive amounts of money on their competitor intelligence by developing a specialized office that does nothing but collect and circulate marketing and competitor intelligence. The employees staffed in this office are rifling through publications, websites, news reports, and other sources looking for pertinent information. They collect this information in a file or database that they share with the marketing manager. It is important to know that information gathering in marketing intelligence is a critical function but is not so critical that illegal actions should be taken to gather the information.

Marketing intelligence can be collected using a few different outlets. First, organizations can utilize documentation and materials that are publicly available. Examples of this type of information would be:

- Government agency publications

- Annual reports

- News reports

- Websites

- Advertisements

- Trade organization sites

- Search engines

- Internet harvesting sites

Another way of collecting information is by simply watching what the competitors do and taking note. Some organizations will purchase a competitor's product and take it apart to reveal its advantages and disadvantages. After noting what works and what does not, the competitor will attempt to improve upon the existing competitor product.

Often people who work with competitors are good sources of competitive information. If a customer works with a competitor frequently, he or she can inform your organization on the latest happenings of the competitor. Sometimes, companies will go as far as sending a "spy" to gather information on competitors. There is obvious ethical question to this method that your organization will need to answer internally before considering this option. Job interviews or discussions with competitor staff may also yield valuable information.

The Process of Marketing Research

The final information category is marketing research. Marketing research focuses on link the consumer or customer to the organization, specifically the marketing manager. Linking the two allows organizations to gather information to help them determine their opportunities and issues, to review marketing actions, understand how well they are performing, and increase comprehension of the marketing process.

Below is a diagram indicating the marketing research process. This process is what marketing researchers follow.

Figure 3.2

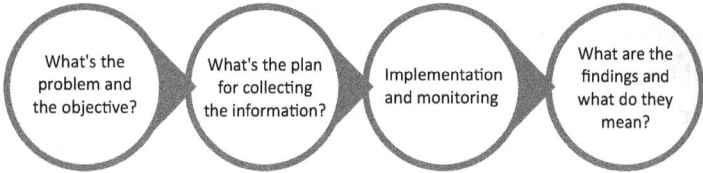

| What's the problem and the objective? | What's the plan for collecting the information? | Implementation and monitoring | What are the findings and what do they mean? |

What's the Problem and the Objective?

The first step in the marketing research process is to ask the question, "What is the problem I am trying to solve and what is my objective?" Clear understanding of the answer to this question by the researcher and the manager are critical to obtaining relevant information that will affect decision making. Some describe this step as the most difficult of all the steps in the process because there are instances where you know the problem, but you do not know its cause. When you have instances such as these, it is helpful to understand the most common objectives for marketing research.

One common objective of marketing research is for exploratory purposes. Essentially, the organization wants information that will help them clarify the problem they are trying to solve and suggest possible causes to test for. Another objective is for descriptive purposes. This research focuses on better detailing the marketing issue, condition, or market. Lastly, researching for casual purposes helps organizations to detect cause and effect relationships when trying to test out possibly causes to an issue.

What's the Plan?

The next step in the marketing research process is to determine the plan of action for collecting the information needed. We first need to understand what our information needs are, so we reference the problem or objective stated in step one and translate that to answer the question, "What's the information needed?" Start your action plan by collecting secondary and primary data. Secondary data is information that is out there, somewhere, but was collected for a different reason. Secondary data can be obtained quickly and cost less to attain. Unfortunately, there are instances where the type of data you are looking for does not exist which presents a problem.

A common source for data for the marketing process include commercial sources such as outside suppliers who sell secondary data reports. Online databases and the internet provide some great resources for conducting searches of secondary data. Primary data is collected specifically for the reason at hand. It includes qualitative and quantitative data. Qualitative looks at a small group of views of the consumer. Quantitative actually looks at a larger group and provides statistics. Primary data can be gathered by simple observation which is called observational research.

Approaches to Research

Observational research consists of observing people, actions, and conditions to gather information. Observing people electronically is a popular approach where organizations use devices such as television (with people meters), checkout scanners, and other single source data systems to conduct observational research. Observational research allows researchers to glean information from the target population that they would not normally share.

Survey research is also another way of gathering primary data. Surveys are best used to collect detailed information. Surveys can be structured or unstructured. Structured surveys are a designed list of questions for respondents. Unstructured surveys can be used during interviewing when the interviewer can modify their questions based on previous responses. Surveys can also be direct or indirect. Direct surveys ask the immediate question at hand. For example, "Why have you stopped shopping at Walmart?" Indirect surveys use indirect questions to come to an answer. An example, "How would you characterize the average Walmart consumer?"

Survey research is very commonly used to collect primary data. The big advantage is that surveys can be flexible. Also, if designed well, surveys can be a quick and low-cost way to collect the data needed. Survey research has a downside as well. People may be unable to answer questions for various reasons or they may choose not to respond all together. People may also make up an answer or try to give the answers they think the interviewer is looking for. Finally, surveys require time from people and in this day and age of multi-tasking, a lot of people do not have the time.

Collecting primary data by delineating between different groups of people, giving them different interventions, and looking for differences is called experimental research. In experimental research, organizations are looking for relationships that have a cause and effect.

Methods of Contact

Research can be done through various contact methods such as mail, telephone, face to face or through the internet. Each method has their advantages and disadvantages. The most commonly used method is through the internet because you can get to a population that you can't get to through mail or telephone. Depending on how it is structured, internet data collecting is quick and relatively easy to do. Below is a table that helps you understand the advantages and disadvantages of the more popular contact methods. Each of the characteristics are measured on a low, medium, high scale.

Table 3.1

	Flexibility	Quantity	Interviewer control	Sample Control	Response speed	Response rate	Cost
Mail	Low	Medium	High	Low	Low	Low	Low
Telephone	Medium	Medium	Medium	High	High	Medium	Medium
Personal	High	High	Low	Medium	Medium	Medium	High
Internet	Medium	Medium	High	Medium	High	Low	High

The best contact method depends on what the researcher is looking for and how much information is needed. There is not a "one size fits all" answer to the best contact method question. It really depends on what will fit for your specific project.

Planning Your Sample

When researchers are developing their plans for market research, they need to determine what the sample of the population looks like that is representative of the whole population they need information from. A sample group is designed to represent the larger group as a whole. When designing these samples, it is helpful to include a few details. First, who will you study? Answer this question carefully as the answer is not always clear. For example, who is the target audience to ask questions about a family car purchase? Is it the husband, wife, both, neither, or someone else?

Next, how many people will you study? You want to make sure you have a large enough sample size to represent the larger population and improve reliability. Sample sizes that are too small can affect the reliability of the results. As a general rule of thumb, if you choose a sample size of slightly less than 1 percent of the larger population, your sample size should be well sized.

Lastly, how will these people be selected? There are all kinds of different ways to select the people in your sample. Probability samples include representatives of each population member and researcher can use statistical analysis to determine confidence level and sample error. Non-probability samples are not measurable by sample error and are less costly and quicker than probability samples.

Research Devices

Research is usually conducted using one of two types of instruments. The first instrument is the questionnaire and is the most commonly used. It is a group of questions that is distributed to people in the sample for their responses. Flexibility is a major advantage of questionnaires because you can ask a question a multitude of ways. The downside is that sometimes questions that should be asked are left out or include questions that are not really needed or obtainable.

When developing questionnaires, it is important to understand the form of the question, so you can get the type of response you are looking for. If you ask an open-ended question, respondents can write freely their answers without any specific set of prescribed answers. Close ended questions give the respondent all of the possible answers and asks the respondent to choose from the preset answers. Questions should be carefully constructed so not to create bias amongst respondents. They should be easy for anyone to read. The questions should generate interest, so respondents are incented to continue filling out the questionnaire.

The other type of instrument is a mechanical instrument. Examples of mechanical instruments may be people meters, pupilometer, or super market scanners. All of these instruments have an automated way to survey respondent interests. People meters are commonly distributed by Nielsen and are attached to TVs to monitor what people are watching. Pupilometers measure eye movements to understand a person's interest based on certain stimuli. Super market scanners track what people are buying.

Present the Plan

After gathering all of the items above, the information should be arranged into a written proposal. There are many elements to a research plan so writing out the proposal helps management get the big picture. The plan should include what the problem is, the objectives, the data included, the sources and methods for the information, and recommendations. Costs should also be included in the plan.

Implement the Plan

Implementing the plan involves gathering and reviewing the information. Gathering information during this phase is generally the costliest part of the research process and has a high risk of error. This phase should be monitored closely to manage cost and manage risk of error. This piece is also very time consuming as researchers have to come through results to tabulate answers and ensure completeness.

Interpreting the Results

The final step is to interpret the findings of the research. At this time, the research is drawing conclusions based on the data and providing them to leadership. It is important to note that conclusions from researchers should not be accepted by managers at face value. Managers are the most familiar with the problem so if something does not seem right, more investigation should take place. Also, the manager should conduct a process of checks and balances to ensure that the process itself was completely correctly and objectively. At the end of the day, the marketing manager is the one who either accepts or denies the conclusions and creates plans based on those conclusions so ensuring accuracy and objectivity is critical. Managers should also be careful not to bring their own biases into the interpretation of the results.

With advances in technology today, more and more organizations are utilizing marketing decision support systems that help marketing managers improve their decision making. These systems include hardware and software that collects the data and helps to interpret it with recommendations.

Characteristics of Valid Market Research

The market research process is a lengthy and complex process. With so many steps and manual work to be done, there are many places where error can occur and invalidate the data. When managers are reviewing the process for validity and substance, they should look at specific characteristics to help them review the data.

Figure 3.3

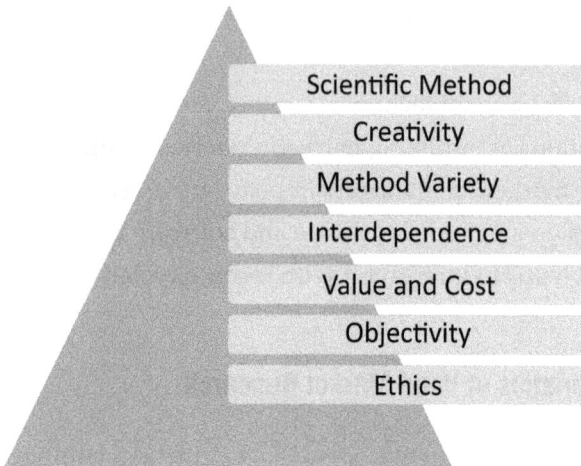

Scientific Method
Creativity
Method Variety
Interdependence
Value and Cost
Objectivity
Ethics

Let's look at these characteristics in a bit more detail.

- **Scientific method**   Good research uses the scientific method; observe, hypothesize, predict, and test.

- **Creativity**   Think outside the box when conducting research. Don't stay behind a desk and develop theories. Get out there with your customer and test ideas real time and in creative ways.

- **Method variety**   Using many methods allow you to validate the data in many ways to increase confidence in the results.

- **Interdependence**   Understanding that data is construed in ways that are reliant upon different models that drive you to specific types of information.

- **Value and cost**   The cost of the information is important but what is the value of the information collected? Did you spend $30,000 on data that seems unreliable and lacks invalidity? Can the manager act on the data presented?

- **Objectivity**   It is important that no bias be involved in interpretation of the data. Data should be reviewed with a questioning attitude to avoid common pitfalls.

- **Ethics**   Was the data collected ethically and will it be used ethically? Do you run the risk of presenting a bad image to consumers due to ethical questions in research?

What is the Demand?

When pulling together information to make marketing decisions, it is important to understand the level of demand in a new and attractive market. Estimating the market demand is an important step that provides supporting information to help organizations make the decision of entering a new market. Demand can be measured and estimated using many characteristics. It can be measured on product levels such as product item, form, line, company sales, industry sales, etc. It can be measured at a space level such as consumer, territory, country, region, etc. It can also be measured on time levels including short, medium, and long range.

Figure 3.4

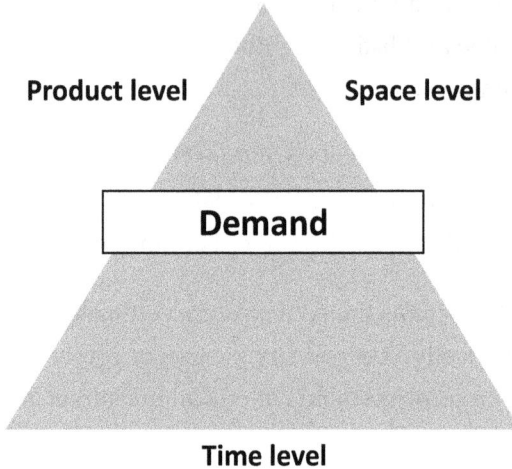

Each level of demand measures a specific item and has its own reason for being. For example, an organization may want to look at short range total demand for a product, so they understand how to plan. Or, an organization may look at long run regional demand for an existing product line to develop a plan for expansion.

Marketing Definitions

There are several terms commonly used in marketing that are important to define for your reference moving forward. This section will provide those definitions. Knowing these definitions is useful for planning.

As mentioned in the introduction, a market includes all buyers and possible purchasers of a product or service. Just as a market is all buyers, an industry is all sellers of a product or service. Buyers in a market are commonly referred to in terms of their level of interest, income and access to the product. If you were to imagine all of the buyers that say they are interested in a product or service, you would be thinking of a potential market. Whereas, an available market is more reflective of current state. Available market are all the buyers who have the three characteristics (interest, income, and access). Taking it a step further, if you think about who you are really focusing your market on, you may disqualify some possible consumers because you are discouraging sales to them. In this case, the buyers that are qualified to be sold the product or service and they have the three characteristics are known as the qualified available market. Let's drill down even further. Your organization may look at the qualified available market and decided to pursue a niche population of that market. The served market is that niche population.

We talked a lot about the market in terms of buyers but what about those who have already bought the product or service? This market is called the penetrated market. Let's look at a couple of diagrams to help us better picture what this looks like.

Figure 3.5

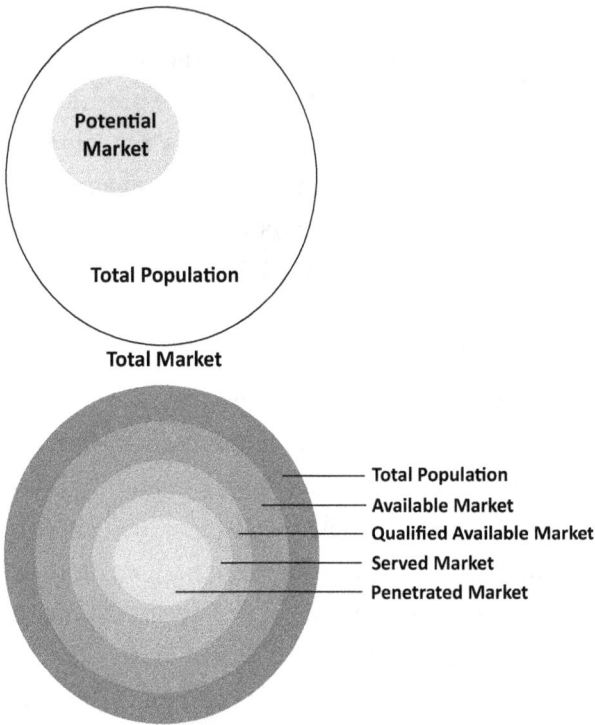

What is the Current Market Demand?

Total market demand, area market demand, actual sales and market shares are areas of current market demand that show the big picture to marketers.

First, total market demand gives a picture of the volume of a product or service the can be purchased using the different aspects of demand – space, product and time. It looks at the target customer group who will purchase. It takes into account the region in which the product will be purchased and the time period in which it will be purchased. All these things are measured specific to a defined level and mix of industry marketing effort. The upper limit to marketing demand, or the level to which if you spend more on marketing it will not increase demand much more, is called market potential. At the opposite end, sales that would occur even if there are no marketing dollars spent is called the market minimum.

Looking at the distance between the market minimum and market potential tells us how sensitive the market is to any marketing efforts. This sensitivity is described by two different types of markets. The expandable market says the size depends on the level of marketing spending. Non-expandable says that marketing spending generates very little demand. In the non-expandable market primary demand is as given. Primary demand is the entire demand for all brands of a product or service. When primary demand is as given, the focus is placed on selective demand or demand for "our" brand of the product or service. All this to say that when marketers estimate total demand, they should be careful to clearly define the situation at hand.

Below is a way organization can estimate total market demand:

$T = b \times a \times m$

T = total market demand

b = number of buyers

a = amount the average buyer purchases per year

m = price per unit

How would you estimate the total market demand in this instance? There are 5 million buyers of books each year. The average buyer purchases 12 books per year. The average price of a book is $10.

5,000,000 x 12 x $10 = 600,000,000

There is also a variation to this equation which is known as the chain ratio method. In this method, you multiply a base number by a chain of adjusting percentages.

The last piece of current market demand is estimating the actual sales and market shares. This can be done by looking at the industry's sales as a whole and seeing what ratio of sales an organization owns. Many companies can actually purchase this type of report rather than spend manpower try to figure it out on their own. Understanding what ratio of the market sales your organization owns versus your competitors is crucial to knowing what your organization's place in the market is.

What Could the Demand be for the Future?

Understanding our current state of demand is an excellent measurement to tell us how we are performing but what about planning for the future? Forecasting looks at a set of conditions and estimates what the demand would be. Forecasting is a challenge because easy forecasting is not accomplished for many products or services. Good forecasting is critical because poor forecasting can lead to surplus inventories, lost sales due to low or no stock, and costly price reductions.

A three-stage process is typically used to help improve accuracy for sales forecasting. First, an organization will complete an environmental forecast. This action is used to try to guesstimate what the future characteristics of the organizational environment might be so planning decisions can be made for the future to deal with the environment of tomorrow. This forecast takes into account things like inflation, unemployment, government expenditures, and other environmental factors. This forecasting gives us a guesstimate of gross national product which will then go into forecasting industry sales. Next, they complete an industry forecast or market forecast. This forecast looks at the market itself and attempts to predict numbers, characteristics and trends. The last stage is the company sales forecast which is where an organization is predicting numbers for their company specifically. This forecast takes into account a specific amount of industry sales.

When forecasting in any of these stages, we are basing our forecast on what trusted sources say, what people are currently doing, and what history shows us. We survey our trusted sources, or buyers, to get their comments. We want to get an idea of what buyers intend to do, a big picture of sales team opinions on what they may do, and expert feedback on what they may do. An organization actually puts a product into a test market when they are trying to figure out what people will do. This is an actual test conducted and used for and indicator of forecasting sales moving forward. Lastly, we look at past history to tell us how the buyers have behaved during specific time periods or seasons to help us forecast.

Figure 3.6

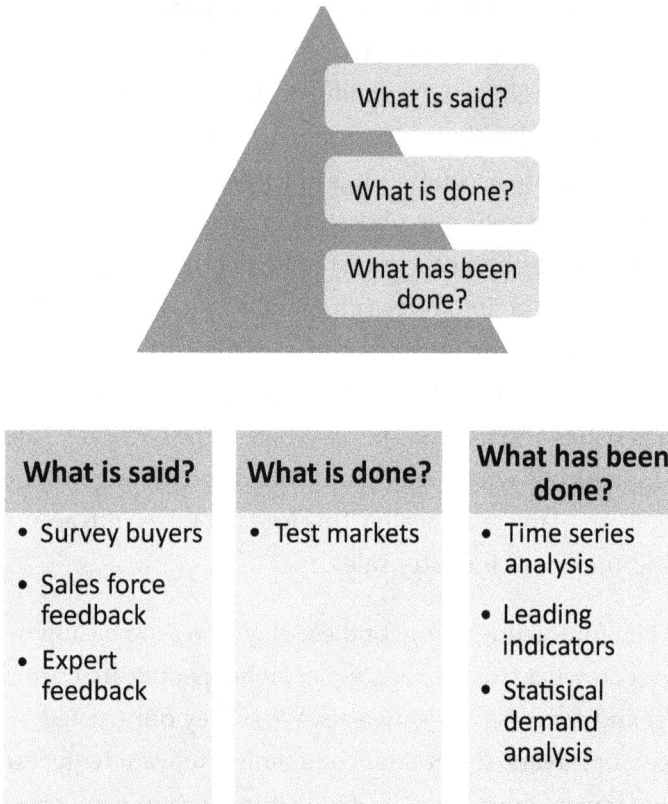

What is said?	What is done?	What has been done?
• Survey buyers • Sales force feedback • Expert feedback	• Test markets	• Time series analysis • Leading indicators • Statisical demand analysis

What is Said?

If we want to know what buyers will do, why not ask them directly? That is what this stage of the process does – surveys buyers directly. One common way of surveying is using a purchase probability scale. This scale asks a question of the buyer and gives them a choice of responses based on their likelihood to purchase.

Below is an example:

How likely are you to purchase a new iPhone in the next six months?

- *No chance*

- *Slight possibility*

- *Fair possibility*

- *Good possibility*

- *Strong possibility*

- *Definitely*

Gathering this information allows companies to anticipate possible shifts in demand and plan accordingly. This can also be used on the business buying side in regard to plant, equipment, and materials acquisitions.

When you can't interview buyers and prospective buyers, you can base forecasting on what the sales team is seeing out in the field. This information can be gathered by territory which makes it useful for planning. The downside is that adjustment has to be made for human error. Sales team members are biased and could lean towards a pessimistic or optimistic side. Don't discount their feedback though. They are closest to the buyer and can see trends in the environment early on. Also, they may be incented to meet what they estimate.

Dealers, suppliers, consultants, marketing associations and many others are known as experts. Expert feedback is commonly used for forecasting. The important thing to remember here is to ensure your organization is not solely reliant on the expert's opinion. Look for supporting data that will help provide more accuracy to their opinion before making plans based on them.

What is Done?

A great indicator of future sales is to look at the buyer's behavior today using test markets. This involves put the product out in a test market to see how well it sells. This is a great tool for new product sales or established product sales that are moving into a new region or territory.

What Has Been Done?

Trend, cycle, period, and unpredictable components make up the time series analysis. Essentially organizations break down sales into these four areas for review and then recombine them to develop their forecast. When organizations detect a long-term pattern of action, either growth or decline in sales, as a result of some kind of change in population, technology or capital, it is known as a trend. A cycle is detected when there are changes in the economy or competitive activity that cause a wavelike movement of sales. Period or seasonality shows a pattern of sales that is consistent within the year. This pattern could be seen in a season or particular segment of time such as hourly, daily, weekly, monthly, yearly, or by season. Lastly, unpredictable components include things like fads, strikes, weather, and other major disturbances in the environment.

Leading indicators have also been used to forecast sales. This means that an organization looks for a correlating indicator in another time series that moves in the same direction but ahead of organization sales. For example, a trim carpentry company may find that its sales increase when housing sales increase in their area.

Lastly, some companies use statistics to analyze past and

future sales. Statistical demand analysis uses statistics to generate data on how important specific factors have historically been on sales, so you can take them into account for future sales. Prices, income, population, and marketing are among the most commonly looked at factors. Statistics can be very complex and challenging so it is imperative that the marketer be very careful in designing, performing, and interpreting the analysis. With the rise of technology, statistical analysis is becoming more and more popular because all of the tedious calculation can be completed by computers.

Ethics in Marketing Research

Over the past several years, researchers have seen survey rates decline due to consumer resentment. Some consumers even refuse to be interviewed because they feel companies misuse the information they provide. The sentiment of "big brother is watching" is rampant in our society today and a reason why people have stopped taking surveys. They are concerned that large organizations are using the data to monitor them and manipulate their buying habits. For the most part, they just see the constant attempts for response to research surveys as an intrusion to their privacy, so they avoid the telephone, email, and mail surveys all together.

Another reason people avoid participating in research is because they are afraid that the feedback will be misused. Essentially, buyers have found that those posing as researchers are really just looking for sales leads.

Chapter Summary

◆ Marketing Information Systems utilizes people, equipment, and procedures to evaluate marketing information for decision makers.

◆ Information is constructed through Internal records, Marketing Intelligence, and Marketing Research.

◆ Marketing Intelligence can be described as information about the current marketing environment and its developments that can help managers create and manage their marketing plans.

◆ A Penetrated Market is a market that has already begun buying the specific type of product or service.

◆ Forecasting is a strong tool for estimating demand, but is highly dependent on what is said, done and has been done.

Chapter 4

Relationships with Customers and Marketing Management

Historically, there has been little need for customer relationship management especially as seen in the marketing sector. Sellers markets weren't required to really please customers because there were monopolies and shortages, so customers accepted what they got. As the tables turned and markets became buyers' markets, customer satisfaction became key because they had a wide array of choices and a multitude of suppliers to choose from. If the customer is not satisfied, they can easily go to a competitor to get their needs met. If sellers want to survive in today's economy, they must make sure their customers are satisfied with their product or services.

Customer Value

Organizations should be customer centered – they must provide the target customer a grander value than competitors. They can do these developing relationships with customers and they must utilize the mechanics of market engineering rather than solely focusing on the engineering of the product itself. Creating customers is an organization's first objective in order to be successful. In order to do this, an organization must understand how the customer makes choices. One answer to this question is that customers consult various marketing offers and choose the one that gives them the best value. Value given to the customer, also known as customer delivered value, is the total customer value minus the total customer cost. Total customer value is the total value observed by the buyer including product, services, personnel, and images. The total customer cost is, in its entirety, the money, energy, intellectual time, and time related to the marketing offer.

Figure 4.1

This is an important equation to know because it can be used to help succeed in selling products and services. The organization can look at improving the total customer value by increasing the benefits of the product, service, personnel or image. It can reduce the total customer cost buy decreasing the energy, time, and intellectual time. Or, it can it can reduce cost of the product or service to help with increasing sales or in the long term reduce operating costs with value passed on to the customer.

Organizations utilize customer value assessments to better understand the customer value by looking at the customer's wants, needs or expectations. The assessment looks at things like:

- Do customers prefer the solution the organization is offering?

- Are customers getting what they want when they want it from the organization?

- Is the financial value attractive that the organization provides?

- Does the customer think the organization is important?

If an organization wishes to deliver a higher value add to the customer, it can lower the price which increases the value delivered to the customer and therefore increases the incentive to purchases. This delivered value is essentially a profit given to the customer.

Some marketers argue that not all buying behavior can be rationalized. In these cases, this type of behavior can be explained by things like:

- Loyalty to long term relationships

- Lowest price seeking

- Low level of funds

Ultimately, buyers operate under different limitations that can affect their behavior that cannot be explained by the model mentioned above.

Customer Satisfaction

Customers development their own judgements of value and what the value of a product or service is to them. Looking at customer satisfaction, they customers actually look at how well a product or service performs for them according to their expectations. If it performs really well, they may be more than just satisfied. If it performs as expected, they may be satisfied. If it performs less than as expected, they maybe unsatisfied. Customers usually base these expectations on:

- Past experience

- Insight from others

- Promises from marketers and/or competitors

Organizations have historically seen customer satisfaction as a delicate dance. If you set expectations low, you could experience issues getting new buyers. If you set expectations too high, you could be setting up customers for disappointment. However, some organizations are willing to take the risk of setting expectations high with the intention of meeting them.

This approach is really using the philosophy of total customer satisfaction. When organizations embrace this philosophy, they rely heavily on the following process.

Figure 4.2

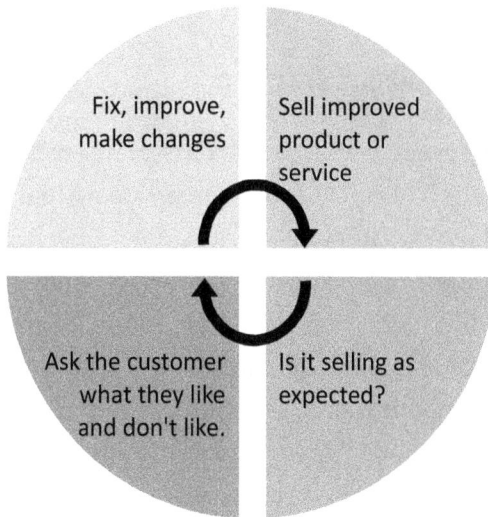

Today's top organizations are looking at customer satisfaction on a regular basis along with customer expectations and perceived performance. When they look at customer satisfaction, the focus is not on past satisfaction scores. What passed as satisfying in previous years may no longer be satisfactory due to changes in competitor performance. As competitors enter new and better products in the marketplace, the standards become higher. Therefore, tracking customer satisfaction on a real-time basis is critical to reaching organizational goals and achieving success for customer centered organizations.

High levels of customer satisfaction are desirable for today's organizations but maximizing that satisfaction is not the objective. Satisfaction can usually be improved by increasing services or lowering the price, but this can have a long-term outcome of lower profits. So, the goal of marketing is to create value to the customer profitably and not increase satisfaction at the expense of other partners.

Customer Satisfaction Tracking

There are several ways to track customer satisfaction. The simplest way is a complaint and suggestion system. You may see suggestion boxes at different organizations where customers can provide comments or complaints on service. Another method is through satisfaction surveys. This method is commonly used at service organizations such as hospitals. Satisfaction surveys give organization a better idea of what is going on with customer satisfaction than complaint and suggestion systems. Organizations distribute surveys on a regular basis for real time feedback and they take action based on feedback. They make changes were needed according to survey response. Ghost shopping is a popular tracking method used in retail stores. People go into an establishment posing as a customer and report back on their experience with great detail about how things went. This can be done internally as well by managers as they walk around and see how customers are being treated. Or, managers can pose as a customer themselves. Lastly, exit interviews are a great way to find out how you can improve. Interviewing customers that are no longer using your products or services gives insight into improvements needed to maintain the customer base.

Providing Satisfaction

Value is provided through the value chain as described earlier in this writing. Customer satisfaction and profitability are closely related to the quality generated and delivered to the customer through the value chain. When there are increased levels of quality, there are also increased levels of customer satisfaction. Customers are willing to pay higher prices for higher quality. This is where Total Quality Management comes in. TQM increases profitability using continuous improvement measures throughout the organization to deliver higher quality products and services. Today, marketing shares the accountability for focusing on high quality. Since customer satisfaction is central to marketing and total quality management there needs to be a strong commitment being an advocate for the customer's satisfaction. Considering an organization that is both quality and customer centered, marketing can have a couple of responsibilities. First, marketing management will take part in the process of developing strategies and procedures that allocate appropriate resources. The main goal is quality excellence. Next, marketing needs to make sure that in addition to quality in the product production as well as quality in marketing.

Historically, marketing has not been thought of as being included in quality projects. Today, marketing is recognized as being close to the consumer, so their participation is key. First, marketing can help pinpoint customer's wants and needs. They can also facilitate communication with customers to ensure product design and production is on point. Next, marketing plays a role at making sure customers' orders are processed correctly and in a timely manner. Marketing facilitates training and technical assistance for the product. Finally, they keep in touch with the customer after they have purchased and used it. This is where we gather information about how satisfied they are and any ideas for future enhancements or fixes for the product.

TQM, as mentioned earlier, has really helped in educating organizations on quality and that it is more than just a well manufactured product. TQM brings home the point that quality goes hand in hand with customer satisfaction. It also helps marketing understand that quality is more than just in their department. It is acquiring, retaining, and satisfying exceptional employees so that the organization can acquire, retain, and satisfy customers.

How Much is a Customer Worth?

How much is a customer worth? This is a critical question to ask when considering how much an organization is willing to spend to improve quality to retain customers and gain new ones. A profitable customer is a customer whose revenues, during a specified period of time, are greater than the organization's costs of marketing, selling, and servicing that customer. For customer profitability, we are not focused on a single transaction but the lifetime revenues and costs. This is termed customer lifetime value – the amount where revenues exceed organization costs over a specified period of time. Measuring customer value and profitability is a challenge because often transactions can be spread across multiple departments. The organizations that have been successful at tracking customer profitability and lifetime value have been surprised at how unprofitable their customers are.

Retaining Customers

When there is high customer turnover, costs are higher than if all customers are retained and no new ones are obtained. Organizations have to take the time to monitor what their customer rate of defection is. The first step in doing this is to state, monitor, and measure the rate of retention. If you are an organization that offers a subscription service, your retention rate may be your renewal rate. Next, the organization should define the different causes for why patients defect and determine which of these can be addressed. An easy way to do this is to conduct a satisfaction study.

When retaining customers, it is important to note that customers do switch providers when they think a better value is out there. Even if they incur high switching costs (i.e. learning a new product, learning a new service), customers will deal with it. There is little research that suggests that incompatibility gives an organization a real advantage at the end of the day. What's more important is to have the best product or service out there and not focus on being first to market or a grand base of customers. Remember, the incompatibility (or high switching costs) outside of purchase price are not as important to the customer as a better offer.

Relationship Marketing

A marketing function where organizations develop, maintain, and improve strong relationships with high levels of value with customers and stakeholders. Notice that the focus is on long term relationships and not transactions. The goal here is to provide value to customers for the long term and term success as long term customer satisfaction.

There are several different relationships that can be developed with customers.

Figure 4.3

Basic	• Product sold by sales person • No follow up
Reactive	• Product sold by sales person • Follow-up left to customer to initiate if there are any issues or questions
Accountable	• Product sold by sales person • Sales person follows up by phone for satisfaction • Sales person asks for suggestions for improvement and any issues
Proactive	• Product sold by sales person • Sales person and/or others in the organization follow up for suggestions for improvement and new products
Partnership	• Product sold by sales person • Organization continuously communicates with all customers to see how value can be better delivered

Organizational relationship marketing planning is related to how many customers it has and their profitability. For example, organizations with low profit margins and few customers will practice a reactive marketing strategy. However, if their number of customers grows to medium or high, they will use a basic marketing strategy. If an organization has a medium profit margin and anywhere from few to medium customers, they will utilize an accountable marketing strategy. But, if their number of customers grows to many, their strategy becomes reactive. The most varying is when there is a high profit margin. The strategy changes with the number of customers. For few customers, it is a partnership strategy. For medium number of customers, it is a proactive strategy and for many customers it is an accountable strategy. As the number of customers increase, the amount of effort that can be put into the relationship marketing strategy lessens.

So how do organizations go about building those bonds with customers? There are three approaches to this.

- Add financial benefits

- Add financial benefits and social benefits

- Add financial, social, and structural benefits

An example of adding financial benefits would be a frequent flyer program where customers can get a free upgrade or free flight with their airline miles. Social benefits happen when an organization builds a personal bond with the customer by understanding their wants and needs and then personalizing products and services to meet those wants and needs. Structural ties are adding something to the product to or service delivered to build a stronger relationship. An example would be how a bank adds an online banking or bill payment solution with their checking accounts free of charge.

To set up a relationship marketing program, a few steps should be followed.

- Clarify which customers you are targeting for relationship management.

- Develop relationship manager roles and assign one to each

targeted customer.

- Ensure the job description of the relationship manager is clearly defined.

- Establish long term customer relationship plans with relationship manager input.

- Develop an overall manager role to manage the relationship managers.

When Do I Use Relationship Marketing?

Since there are different types of customers, there are different customers that are appropriate for relationship marketing. Customers that are short term and can easily switch to a better offer with little effort or amount spent, are better served with transactional marketing. Customers that are more long term and have high switching costs are ideal for relationship marketing.

Relationship Management

Relationships with customers are typically managed with customer relationship management. This is a strategy to solidify our relationships with our clients. This system reduces cost, time, enhances productivity and profitability in an organization. The system collects all the data from all over the organization regarding our clients and places them in a central location that employees can access when needed. This system not only collects data on our existing clients, but it also captures our relationships with prospective clients.

An effective customer relationship management system has the following features:

- Identifies client needs including likes and dislikes.

- Documents client response activities to any inquiries or requests. This includes both positive and negative interactions with the client.

- Measures the client's level of satisfaction by feedback from the client.

- Measures the client's level of loyalty by looking at whether the client would recommend our organization, how often they come for return business, are they going to competitors for any needs, etc.

- Promotes customer retention.

- Tracks customer complaints and how they were handled.

- Delivers information and services through customer service.

Customer relationship management systems are important because they provide a wealth of knowledge on clients in one spot that can easily be analyzed and acted upon. It reduces redundancies between departments since each department is not managing their own customer files. The system provides a mechanism to review the progress you have made with a customer. You can look at their full history with the company. Customer relationship systems are also very cost effective and helpful in tracking new relationships with potential customers.

Figure 4.4

Customer
Needs

Customer
Service

Customer
Response

**Customer
Relationship
Management**

Customer
Complaints

Customer
Satisfaction

Customer
Retention

Customer
Loyalty

Defining Customer Relationship

Dictionary.com defines relationship as the way in which two or more people are connected. Relationships evolve over time. Think about the relationships in your life. Your best friend was not your best friend the first day you met. The relationship evolved over time. The same concept applies for customer relationships.

Below is an outline of the evolution relationships typically go through.

Figure 4.5

Exploration > Awareness > Expansion > Commitment > Dissolution

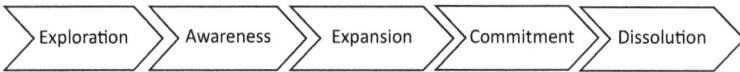

- **Exploration** The prospective client is investigating or testing your organization's capabilities and performance. They are comparing to industry standards and performance to competitors. At the same time, they are looking at the product's or brand's usefulness and asking, "Is this really worth it?"

- **Awareness** The prospective client has an understanding of the motivational values of the organization or their products.

- **Expansion** The customer puts their faith in your organization and agree to do business with you. A relationship of interdependence is formed. At this time, expansion of services and products is a great possibility.

- **Commitment** Your organization now understands what business rules your client operates under. You work to follow those roles and not just meet their needs but go above and beyond.

- **Dissolution** The relationship ends with the client. The customer no longer needs the services your organization offers and begins to look for better perspectives.

Types of Customers

Since customers are such a critical part of an organization's business, it is important to understand that customers can be categorized into groups to better demonstrate their value. In order to properly manage your customers, identifying which group your customer belongs in essential. The categories of groups the customer can fall into are as follows:

Figure 4.6

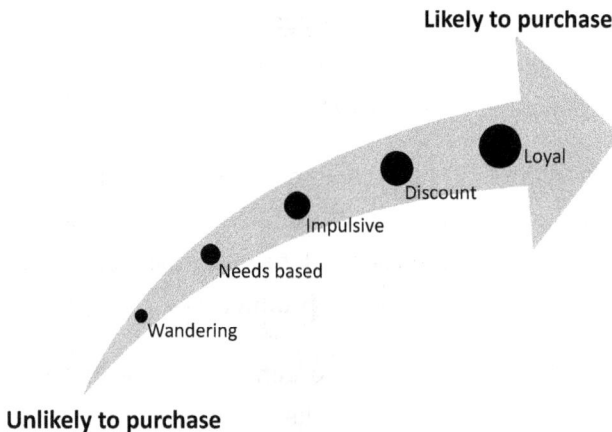

Likely to purchase

Loyal

Discount

Impulsive

Needs based

Wandering

Unlikely to purchase

- **Loyal customers**   Loyal customers are ones that will act as advocate for your organization. They refer customers to you and they act as references to contact for prospective customers. These customers repeatedly contact your organization for business, so it is imperative that you stay in touch with them regularly. These customers expect prompt response and attention and recognition of their loyalty to you.

- **Discount customers** Discount customers may visit you frequently but only when you are offering a discount on services. In fact, the better the discount, the more likely they are to purchase from you. Beware of these customers because there is a risk that they will quickly jump to a competitor if a better discount is offered.

- **Impulsive customers** These customers are driven by the urge to buy. They don't necessarily have a particular need they need to meet or a product to buy but they have the urge to buy. These customers can prove challenging because they don't know what they want so it is difficult to pinpoint what they may purchase. The good thing about these customers is that if you are able to find something that peaks their interest, there is a high probability that these customers will purchase a lot.

- **Need based customers** These customers have a specific need they are seeking to fill you're your organization. They tend to purchase a specific product and nothing more. It is difficult to transition these customers over to purchasing other products in your product line. These types of customers are not necessarily loyal to your organization so if they experience a negative interaction, they may look for other prospects.

- **Wandering customers**   These customers are window shoppers and are the least profitable. They are not really sure what they want to buy and are really just gathering information on products for comparison and needs analysis.

Customer Orientation

Another aspect of customers that you should be aware of is their orientation. What are they most concerned about? Knowing this will allow you to better sell to the customer as well as meet their customer service needs.

- **Cost oriented**   These customers are most concerned about cost even if they have to sacrifice efficacy, performance or quality. These customers typically end up buying the lowest cost product which sometimes leaves them with a loss. They are also quick to blame the supplier when a product they purchased failed rather than looking at the low cost they paid resulting in lower quality. These customers also are known to purchase second hand products and expect them to work as new as well as use local vendors to fix products at lower cost and lesser quality. Both of these expectations result in a failure of the product and the customer turns to the supplier to fix the issue. Therefore, these customers can be very costly.

- **Value oriented**   These customers are looking for the most efficient and high performing products. They are willing to invest higher dollars for the value they receive from a longer running product. In fact, these customers recognize that making a premium investment could result in cost savings in the future, so they are willing to spend the money. Since these customers will spend money for quality products, they tend to be satisfied customers with good relationships with their suppliers.

- **Technology oriented** These customers look for the best technology regardless of cost, quality, or performance. Their outlook is that technology is changing so often that it is in their best interest to stay with the latest technology will help them sustain productivity. Suppliers that focus on frequently releasing the latest and greatest technologies, this is their ideal customer. They are innovative and interested in trying the newest thing out. These customers are typically satisfied customers and have good relationships with their suppliers due to frequent referrals.

Ensuring Quality Customer Relationships

Your organization needs customers in order to sustain everyday business and grow. Therefore, it is vitally important that you take time to examine your relationships with your customers and ensure that they are beneficial for both parties. Most important to a good customer relationship is providing quality goods and services efficiently and effectively. If you can demonstrate to your customer that you can do this better than your competitors, you can win a trustworthy and loyal relationship with a customer. Trust in the relationship gives confidence and security to both parties. Commitment indicates a mutual long-term relationship where both parties work together to uphold the relationship.

Other characteristics of a high-quality relationship are:

- **Courtesy**   Even when a customer becomes annoyed and even rude due to different reasons, it is imperative that the supplier keep their cool. Remaining calm and sympathizing with the issue will help in driving customer satisfaction.

- **Availability**   Some customers prefer to speak to a person rather than through email, voicemail, or electronic responses. Therefore, it is ideal to have a human contact that they can easily get in touch with should they have questions or concerns. This also helps with developing a relationship with the customer that is an emotional bond that helps to drive more business.

- **Responsive**   Prompt response and follow-up to questions and concerns goes a long way in a customer relationship. Lack of response and follow-up can also break a customer relationship and cause them to go to another vendor.

- **Intelligent**   Customers are looking for good deal including discounts and reasonable prices. Suppliers should be strategic in their ability to offer discounted prices to customers to avoid the customer going to a competitor for a better price.

- **Futuristic**   Try to stay up to date with technological changes. As technology evolves, some services and products will become obsolete. Also, if you aren't careful, competitors will develop solutions and services that are more compatible with newer technologies resulting in customers going to the competitor.

Measuring Customer Relationships

How do you quantify your relationships with your customers rather than it being a subjective feeling? Understanding the strength of the relationships you have with your customers helps you plan your next steps to take. Strengthening relationships means that you want to do activities that will add to long term success rather than just short-term wins with the customer. Essentially you are investing in customer success instead of customer support.

Customer success takes into account the long-term relationship. It works proactively anticipate issues and needs before the customer voices them. The goal is to help the customer get as much value from the product or service as they can. We want to help the customer generate revenue with our product.

Customer support focuses on the short term. It is reacting to customer concerns or issues as they come up. The main goal is to address the issue occurring with the product. This does not help the customer generate revenue.

Figure 4.7

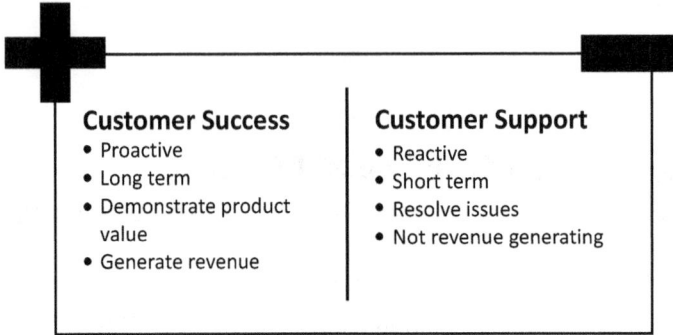

Customer Success
- Proactive
- Long term
- Demonstrate product value
- Generate revenue

Customer Support
- Reactive
- Short term
- Resolve issues
- Not revenue generating

As we look at measuring customer relationships, we want to put our primary focus on measuring customer success. There are several customer success metrics that are being measured in various industries today. Let's take a look at some of the more popular ones.

Churn

Your customer churn rate is defined as the percentage of customers who decide to discontinue use of your product during a specific period of time. There are actually three different types of churn rate that organizations typically calculate on a monthly basis. The first is the customer churn rate previously described. Next, is the gross dollar churn rate which is the percentage of your total revenues that are lost because your customer downgrades to a less expensive option. Third, is the monthly recurring revenue churn (aka net MRR churn) which is the net dollar churn, but it also takes into account the gains that come from customers who purchase additional or upgrade their products.

Figure 4.8

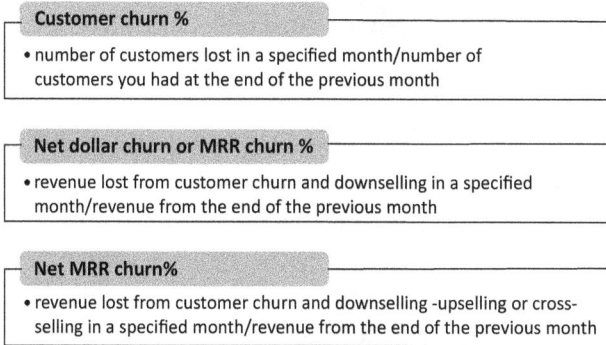

Once you have collected these numbers, what does it all mean? Let's take a look at a graph comparing the three types of churn in a sample business.

Figure 4.9

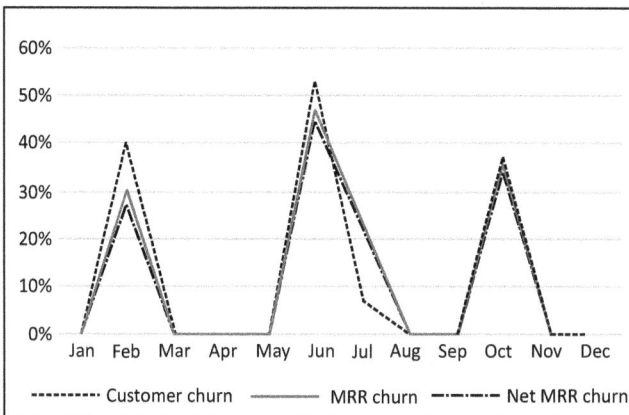

When you look at this chart, you can see that you cannot see the entire picture just by looking at customer churn. If you look at July, you see that the customer churn rate was only 7%. That sounds good, right? Looking at the MRR churn we see that it is 25% which is rather large indicating that a customer left us who was paying us high dollars. Essentially, this shows us how the dissolution of one high paying customer can really affect our business.

Organizations usually set a goal for a customer churn rate below 5%, an MRR churn rate below 1% if they choose to be best-in-class, and a net MRR churn rate of anything -%.

You can gather more information by looking at the actual dollars as well. When you look at dollars, you are putting an actual amount to your churn rates which can indicate to you just how bad your issue is. For example, if you have a small customer base, the loss of one customer can fluctuate the numbers significantly when you look at percentages. When you look at the actual dollars, you see a better picture that can help you determine if this is really an issue you need to work on.

Expansion Revenue

Expansion revenue is another measurement that is helpful to look at when judging the success of your customer relationships. It gives you an idea of the percentage of new revenue that is coming from your existing customers. Where churn measures for retention, expansion measures how well you are able to get your client to grow with your products and solutions.

Measuring expansion revenue on a monthly basis is called expansion MRR. Calculate expansion MRR as follows:

Figure 4.10

> **Expansion MRR**
> • new revenue from upselling and cross-selling in a specified month/
> revenue you had at the end of the previous month

What does expansion MRR tell you about the bigger picture of your organization? Take a look at the graph below.

Figure 4.11

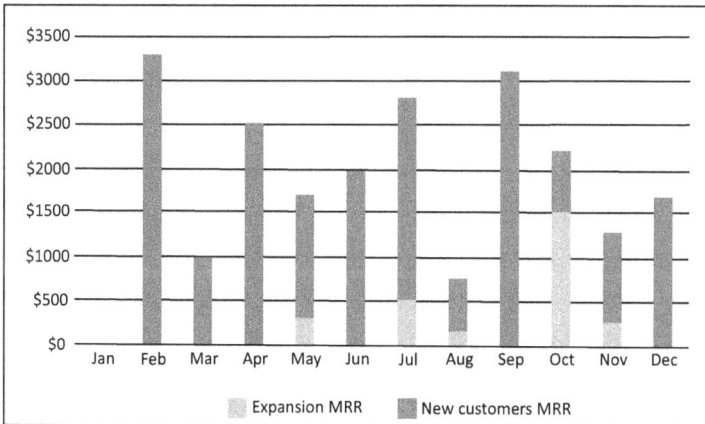

The dark grey bars are sales achieved by the sales team. The orange bars indicate how well you are doing with your customer or your customer success. In the ideal scenario, the expansion MRR is so large that a negative net MRR churn rate is achieved. When this is accomplished, you can grow your revenue even if you cannot get new customers.

The typical goal for expansion MRR in most industries is to offset the churn rate with the expansion MRR and make the MRR churn negative.

Customer Satisfaction

We have looked at metrics that tell us what the customer's actions have been. We know if they have been leaving us or if they have been buying more from us. The gap we have is understanding how the customer is feeling towards our products and company. If you can identify customers whose feelings are not satisfactory, your organization can develop plans to address their concerns and put the relationship in good standing.

Net Promoter Score

Net promoter score is widely used to measure customer satisfaction today. It is a very simple tool to use in that you ask the customer one question – "How likely are you to recommend our product/service/organization to your friends?" The customer chooses a number between 0 and 10. 0 indicates unlikely to recommend at all and 10 igndicates will definitely recommend. The responses are gathered and categorized into three groups:

- 0-6 = Detractors, people who will not recommend your product and may even give your product bad reviews to others

- 7-8 = Passives, people who think the product is ok but probably will not be an active advocate of how great your products are

- 9-10 = Promoters, people who are very happy with your products and will refer your products to their friends and family

Net Promoter Score (NPS) is calculated as follows:

Figure 4.12

> **Net Promoter Score**
> - % promoters - % detractors

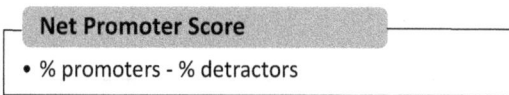

NPS is a great indicator for your potential for growth. It also forecasts your customer loyalty. Your goal is to move your passive scorers to promoters. Detractors are typically more difficult to move so most companies focus on their passive scorers to improve their customer loyalty and therefore potential for growth.

NPS goals vary by organization and industry. 50 is typically viewed as good but it is recommended to look at NPS scores of your competitors for comparison. For example, if my organization manufactures mp3 players, I may strive for an NPS score of 90 since Apple's latest score was 89.

Customer Satisfaction Score (CSAT)

When you look at the customer satisfaction score, you are focus more on their short-term happiness with your product or solution. At the time of taking the survey, how satisfied was the customer with your solution?

In a CSAT survey, there is usually a question that asks, "What is your overall satisfaction with (product/service/ organization)?" The customer is asked to rate from 1 to 5 where 1 is very unsatisfied, 2 is unsatisfied, 3 is neutral, 4 is satisfied, and 5 is very satisfied. The surveys are collected and feedback from this question calculated into a percentage. The end result is a percentage of customers that answered either satisfied or very satisfied.

Figure 4.13

Customer Satisfaction Score (CSAT)

• % of customers who responded satisfied and 5 very satisfied

If you received a score 0f 75%, it would mean that 75 out of the 100 customers who took the survey were satisfied or very satisfied.

A common goal for CSAT in most industries is 80%.

Chapter Summary

◆ In order to create customers, organizations must create Value called Customer Delivered Value.

◆ Customer Satisfaction is based on past experiences, insight from others, and promises from marketers and/ or competitors.

◆ Total Quality Management increases profitability using continuous improvement measures throughout the organization to deliver higher quality products and services, thus improving customer satisfaction.

◆ The Customer Worth, or Lifetime Value, is based on the collective revenues compared to the organizations costs to sell/market the product.

◆ Relationship Marketing: A marketing function where organizations develop, maintain and improve strong relationships with high levels of value with customers and stakeholders.

◆ Relationships with customers are classified as either Basic, Reactive, Accountable, Proactive, or a Partnership.

◆ Customer Relationship Management focuses on customer loyalty, retention, satisfaction, response, ʹ complaints, service, and needs.

◆ The three types of customer orientations are Cost (pricing over all traits), Value (most efficient and high performing), and Technology.

◆ The five characteristics for quality customer relationships are Courtesy, Availability, Responsive, Intelligent, and Futuristic.

◆ Customer relationships are measured through success and support.

◆ Customer Churn Rate is the percentage of customers who decide to discontinue use of the product.

◆ Expansion Revenue depicts the percentage of new revenue coming from existing customers.

Chapter **5**

Digital Marketing

Everyone thinks they know what digital marketing means or, at least, have an inkling of what it means. Gone are the skeptics unsure if digital marketing was actually a potent marketing plan or a mere fancy term to use during meetings. Marketers have now come to understand the concept and we can't shake the feeling that we should be doing more.

Digital marketing is defined as the use of digital technologies to carry out the marketing cycle. Simply put, it is marketing done through digital platforms, as against the former, now near-obsolete, means of marketing. The increasing usage of digital devices has made it absolutely necessary to embrace and fully maximize the benefits proposed via this medium.

Digital marketing is carried out via a number of channels, each of which can, through a digital network, create, hasten and communicate the value of products or contents from origin (perhaps a manufacturer or wholesaler) to a consumer stop (be it a final consumer or retailer). The development of digital marketing over the years has incorporated several new channels of propagating information, some of which are pay-per-click, search engine optimization, mobile apps and many more.

Unlike the first impression of many marketers, digital marketing is not limited to online networks. It is as well possible via offline channels. In this blog, our expert digital marketers have explained the channels through which you may access digital marketing. Note that these channels are broadly categorized into hard and soft skills.

Hard Skills in Digital Marketing

These refer to the core channels through which digital marketing is possible. In this piece, we'll be discussing the most effective six:

Search Engine Optimization (SEO)

The basic concept behind search engine optimization is simple, but could be very tricky. The internet's greatest strength is its worst failing as well. As a huge dumping ground, any person with a digital device and connection can post anything online. Consequently, that makes it very difficult to stand out amongst the mass heaps of junk and gems.

In 2016, verified statistics showed that 2 million blog posts were published by WordPress users everyday. That meant 24 posts were created every second. Forward to 2019, the figure has nearly doubled, with key stats verifying that at least 35 Word Press posts were updated per second.

This means that at least 175 posts were published as you read the above paragraph. And that's for WordPress users only.

Considering other blogging platforms, we could be looking at a figure tripling the count above.

How then do you stand out in such a crowded subway?

Search engine optimization helps your contents rank higher in search results under organic listings (free searches). To break it down, proper use of SEO ensures that your pages appear on the first page results on search engines. As already mentioned, the internet offers thousands of information about a single inquiry and in this age which impatience is the day's order, no net user is willing to click on 'more results' or 'next page' when using a search engine, say Google.

To begin with, Google is the most used search engine, accounting for 75% of web searches according to verified metrics. Coupled with the fact that the first 5 links in a search get 67% of clicks, you may just start to understand why you have to appear in the first page.

Google probably has over 250 factors it uses to rank your page, no one knows for sure. However, what we are clear of is that certain keywords play a very important role in SEO. Google is tailored to serve users and hence always delivers results it considers most suitable for a query. That is, you could write a blog about cars, add useful keywords about universities and rank 1st or 2nd on search queries regarding universities. Quite straightforward and maybe dumb, right?

This however goes wrong eventually. Offended web users could report your page to Google and get you blacklisted and that just about spells the end. It you are uninterested in long-term usage and are merely concerned with quick gains, you may just use effective keywords with no contents. This is often termed black hat SEO.

If you are interested in maintaining your page for long then, you must create helpful contents and use the right keywords. This amounts to white hat SEO. Creating contents can be complicated sometimes, so you may have to settle for a balance between the two: Grey Hat SEO.

Pay-Per-Click (PPC)

You have probably heard of this before. Or you even have an idea how it works but are unsure how to start. A PPC is a digital marketing model that requires websites to pay referrals on every click their ads get. The referrals, in most cases, are popular search engines, such as Google and Bings. They can also be other related sites that have a wider traffic. Say, for example, you're starting out a fashion blog, you could place ads on other fashion blogs that are already well established and hence generates more traffic than you currently do. For each click that your ads get, you have to pay the website on which you have placed the advert. In other words, it's buying visits to your sites instead of earning them normally.

As already said, the most used form of PPC is search engine advertising. Via this option, you can bid for top spot in results to search queries pertaining your offers or contents. When you use this medium, your website or blog is shown as a sponsored link in search results. On every click your link enjoys through the sponsored link, you have to pay a token to the referring engine. When PPC is working appropriately, then the fee paid is often insignificant as it is very little if compared to the profits generated from the clicks.

Creating an effective PPC strategy requires more than just paying though. You must research and offer the right keywords to your referral engine or website in order to generate clicks. Your keywords must be arranged intelligently. More importantly, your PPC landing page (the page users are directed to upon clicking your links) must be optimized for conversion. If users are satisfied with your links, Google charges you less than normal as you're helping in return. This consequently means more profit for you.

To create a useful PPC campaign, the following have to be considered:

- **Keyword**   ensure you use the right keywords, develop tight keyword groups and common ad text

- **Landing page**   see that your landing page is attractive enough to keep users surfing upon landing. Content must be relevant, clear, helpful and persuasive

- **Score**   your score is how Google grades your keywords and landing page. You must have a quality score so as to enjoy more clicks for lesser fees

- **Creativity**   your designs have to be pleasant to the eye. You may use special tools to generate important designs or hire a professional to handle the visual aspect

Digital Display Advertising

Visuals catch one's attention faster and leave more remarkable impressions. Digital display advertising is primarily visuals. It is done in form of banners, whether images or texts, and strategically placed in certain pages or social media platform. Display adverts may be in several forms, but it all comes down to the same fundamentals.

Display ads work just as PPC does, albeit in this instance, the emphasis is on graphics. You can use a number of platforms to place display ads, although the most popular is Google AdWords. There are no limits to the formats of adverts you may place on these platforms. The only restriction would be the size. Google AdWords, for example, recommends the following sizes:

Top performing ad sizes

- 300 x 250 – Medium Rectangle
- 336 x 280 – Large Rectangle
- 728 x 90 – Leaderboard
- 300 x 600 – Half Page
- 320 x 100 – Large Mobile Banner

Regional ad sizes

- 240 x 400 – Vertical Rectangle
- 980 x 120 – Panorama
- 250 x 360 – Triple Widescreen
- 930 x 180 – Top Banner
- 580 x 400 – Netboard

Other supported ad sizes

- 320 x 50 – Mobile Leaderboard

- 468 x 60 – Banner
- 234 x 60 – Half Banner
- 120 x 600 – Skyscraper
- 120 x 240 – Vertical Banner
- 160 x 600 – Wide Skyscraper
- 300 x 1050 – Portrait
- 970 x 90 – Large Leaderboard
- 970 x 250 – Billboard
- 250 x 250 – Square
- 200 x 200 – Small Square
- 180 x 150 – Small Rectangle
- 125 x 125 – Button

Pros of Display Advertising

The top importance of display adverts is its ability to reach a wide range of users within a short period of time. Google AdWords is an impressive platform, offering millions of potential customers on every display ad. This aside, digital display advertising is very flexible. This means that it can be easily created. There are few restrictions with the forms of a display ad.

Importantly, display ads can easily be kept track of. Every click and conversion are recorded as they occur, giving you the opportunity to know the state of the ad at all times.

Cons of Display Advertising

The wide availability of display ads could be a disadvantage in some cases. As display ads are available almost on every page while browsing, people have started to develop a perceived blindness towards it. This is further worsened by the presence of ads blocker in popular browsers. As far back as 2015, 45 million US surfers were using ad blockers and this figure has only increased with time. It has therefore become very relevant to design catchy, enticing graphics.

Email Marketing

You might have heard from several people that emails are becoming quickly obsolete and have now been replaced by the faster, more direct medium, which is chatting. Before you believe this popular opinion, you may want to ask yourself how many official business discussions or transactions you have completed via chat. Have you ever submitted a job proposal via Facebook or WhatsApp chat? Your answer is most likely no. There, you have your answer. We may assume that postal mailing is dead, but not emailing.

Email marketing is self-explanatory as it sounds. It is a form of digital marketing that involves sending messages to prospects and customers via electronic mail. Over the years, email marketing has been a huge source of revenue to many establishments. For example, Traffic and Conversion Summit was launched in 2009 with just 258 attendees. With the proper use of email marketing, this figure had bulged to 4500 in 2017. What's more, T&C realized above $20 million revenue from email marketing in a single year.

As attractive as email marketing appears, it is as well dangerous and could cripple a firm if not done rightly. Quickly think back: how many promotional mails have you replied to in your inbox? This becomes worse if the mail shows up under the spam folder.

Email marketing has an unbelievable ROI of 4400%, that is an expected return of $42 on every $1 spent. But as already mentioned, email marketing must be done well to make profits. So how is it done?

Getting a list of emails to send messages to starts the cycle. This can be easily done via any of the email generators we have online. What matters most is how the bait is taken. A lead magnet would do very well to get your mails positive considerations. A lead magnet is a reward you give in exchange for messaging a prospect. It doesn't have to cost anything; it could be a document, some helpful stats, mp3 file, short video, webinar, free quote and many more.

For example, you message a prospective customer on a product related to heart issues, it would do you very well to attach a free PDF file that gives some information on cardiology. This way, the prospect is likely to open your message and trust you due to the offer you've made.

Email generators are not advisable. You can place your lead magnet in certain positions on your website so as to get visitors to give their email addresses in exchange for the free offer. With adequate traffic and a well-designed lead magnet, you are sure to own a mailing list of people who already know and have interest in what you offer.

Social Media Marketing

Social media marketing is the art of marketing goods and products via social media. The huge number of users across social media platforms has made social media marketing very appealing and effective.

Initially, social media marketing was just publishing posts and championing ad campaigns, but all has changed with time. Gone are the days when all you had to do was create a post on an official page and organize paid ads.

Social media platforms, such as Twitter and Facebook, are very effective in bringing customers close to businesses. On any of the two, followers can express their opinions about your brand and this will be helpful in knowing the next steps to take. You now have to monitor conversations and provide responses to important mentions.

The availability of social media analytics makes marketing easier. With analytics, businesses can make analysis of their reaches and engagements. The successfulness of a campaign can now be easily determined and measured.

Social media marketing is set on five fundamental pillars, which are:

- **Strategy**   This is of course very important before starting your social media marketing. Before any campaign, you should have a definite reason for its use. Your marketing campaign can be for several reasons. It could be for creation of awareness, generation of sales and website traffic, development of a customer support platform and a channel through which brand engagements can be drawn and pursued. This aside, you have to select a suitable platform from the popular ones available. You can choose from Facebook, Instagram, Twitter, YouTube, Pinterest, Snapchat and LinkedIn.

- **Planning and Publishing**   Social media marketing requires you to have a solid online presence. More than 2 billion people use the social media, so when you publish on it, yout brand is exposed to a very wide audience within a short while. Publishing on social media can be a post, an image, animation or video. It must however be planned ahead so as to make it meaningful. You have to publish at the right time as well.

- **Engagements**   With the ideal strategy and relevant publishing, your brand is assured of a rise in recognition and conversations. Your followers will like your posts, air their opinions about your services and participate in ongoing activities. To monitor engagements, you may have to use special tools designed specifically for the purpose. Of course, you may decide to use the traditional method of going through mentions and convos, and that could work fine.

- **Analytics**   Analytics help to analyze the performance of your social media marketing. Whether you're publishing or making engagements, it is necessary to know how things are going. Analytics will help you to know if your strategy is working as it should be and if you're publishing appropriate contents. You can always get in-depth analysis of performance by using tailored tools of the platform you're on.

- **Advertising**   Having satisfied the four fundamentals highlighted above, the next core you want to explore is social media advertising. Via ad campaigns, you have the opportunity to reach a very wide audience. For a token, your brand or product is advertised to users of the platform. Instead of reaching your followers only, you have the chance to advertise yourself to a bigger range of users, depending on the campaign plan you pay for.

Mobile Marketing

Mobile marketing gets far less applause than it deserves. The effects of mobile marketing are either ignorantly overlooked or deliberately unappreciated. As far back as 2014, mobile users were more than PC users. More than 79.9% of internet users do so via a smartphone, be it an Android or iPhone.

The remarkable fact about mobile marketing is that, unlike all other channels, it still functions without the internet. On every mobile, whether smart or not, there are two basic apps to carry out mobile marketing: calls and text messages.

That brings us to cold calling. Cold calling is the act of calling someone with whom you have had no previous contact in order to market a brand or product. According to stats, marketers make 52 calls and average 3 buyers daily. That's about 17:1. It's not an effective method as social media or email marketing is, but it's worth something.

Texting has recorded more success than cold calling. This is because every text is guaranteed a read within 3 minutes of receival under normal circumstances. What makes texting more appealing to cold calling is that you do not have to worry about the prospect's mood. All you have to do is send the message and leave a call-to-action at the end.

To leverage text messaging, you may offer special rewards in exchange for a response. It could be in form of a coupon code, special deals or offers. For example, DVD rental service, Red Box accumulated over 400, 000 new customers and sent 1.5 million text messages within 10 days. Prospects who texted 'DEALS' to 727272 were afforded a gamble in form of a discount that could fall anywhere between $0.10 and $1.50.

Another way to use text messaging is to send notifications to customers when updates are available. Walmart, for example, alerts customers when their orders are ready for acquisition. The campaign has been very successful: sending a billion text messages is more than enough evidence.

You can use mobile marketing through the internet as well. To start, you have to optimize your landing page for mobile devices. Contents on your website must be instantly useful and captivating. You may use high quality texts and brilliant graphics to make it worthwhile. You are advised to keep things simple however as a second delay decreases customer satisfaction and reduces conversion rates.

Every function on your website or marketing campaign must be optimum for mobile users, be it the CTA button, email contacts, social media platform and many more. Would you believe that the average person checks his mobile more than 150 times daily? The possibilities available are just endless.

Analytics

Analytics is concerned with performance measurement and assessment. Whereas, all other aspects of digital marketing highlighted herein are practiced achieving one or two purposes, analytics is done to know if the set machineries are functioning as they should. Analytics, for example, will be useful in an SEO campaign to determine the effectiveness of the keywords and other cogent components. The same applies to the various arms of digital marketing.

Aside the basic sales and lead generation applications, analytics can be used to realize and understand customer preferences and priorities. Take for example social media campaigns. Analytics will help to identify the preferences of followers: do they prefer visual manifestations to written expressions?

The introduction of softwares, such as search engines, paid search and SEO has made analytics far more precise and helpful. But for all of the benefits posed by this monitoring function, some stakeholders decry its usage.

Importance of Analytics

Digital marketing analytics, web analytics, in particular, offer business owners the platform to monitor how each dollar is spent, consequently helping to make every penny worthy of cause.

The concept behind analytics is simple: if the cash spent on an investment is more than the amount received in return, then it isn't worth it and should be discarded.

It's only logical that a business who knows how its investments are handled and the returns made on each investment will outgrow competitors and manage resources better.

Soft Skills in Digital Marketing

Soft skills are as important as hard skills, although does not require any technical knowledge. This is the aspect of digital marketing that deals with the human personality. There are several soft skills to possess in order to be successful as a digital marketer. We'll be looking at some of the most significant below:

- **Tenacity**   This should top the list. As a digital marketer, you must be able to remain motivated even without favorable results. If you give up easily or are quickly bored by processes, digital marketing might not be the field for you. For example, an update might ruin all your efforts on increasing the rank of a website and you'd have to start again. On every day, there's a new thing to try and that's what keeps things worthwhile.

- **Humility to Listen and Learn**   This is of course a skill necessary in every sphere of life. As a digital marketer, you have to be willing to listen to and learn from others when necessary. You could be wrong on a prospect and it is only right that you learn when you should. Without the willingness to listen and learn, you'll be making countless mistakes you could have avoided.

- **Keen on Research**   This is an area you must be abundant in. A digital marketer must have a keen eye for research. Think about it. Hard skills are constantly updated, and new methods incorporated. Without an interest in research, you will be championing several poor and ineffectual marketing campaigns. If you cannot make research, how then would you strategize, plan, publish,gain prospects, design posts and so many more?

Just how?

- **Versatility**   Your ability to adapt to different work situations is relevant to being a successful digital marketer. This is because you might have to work on diversifying assignments. This week, you may be revitalizing the SEO of a website while next week might see you handling the social media platforms of a brand. You have to be adaptable to any situation.

- **Multitasking**   This skill cannot be overemphasized. You must be able to handle several tasks simultaneously without making mistakes. Put in mind that a particular assignment could require more than two hard skills and you must be able to handle all at the same time.

Bottom Line

From all indication, digital marketing is the future. In fact, it is the present. As it stands, YouTube makes more revenue and give more results than any TV adverts. No one is interested in huge billboards while in a vehicle anymore. The next time you're in a car, you may look around to compare the number of those staring out the window and those operating their mobile devices. Pretty alarming difference, you will see. Digital marketing has come to stay and it is recommended that you make the switch very soon.

Chapter Summary

◆ Digital Marketing is the use of digital technologies to carry out the marketing cycle. It is marketing done through digital platforms.

◆ Search Engine Optimization (SEO) is a method which helps your content rank higher in search results under free listings.

◆ Pay Per Click (PPC) is a digital marketing model that requires websites to pay referrals on every click their ads get.

◆ Digital Display Advertising is visuals done in the form of banners and strategically placed on certain pages or social media platforms.

◆ Email Marketing is a form of digital marketing that involves sending messages to customers or prospects via email.

◆ Social Media Marketing is the art of marketing goods and products via social media.

NOTES